THE JUNGLE DOCTOR

THE JUNGLE DOCTOR

THE ADVENTURES OF AN
INTERNATIONAL WILDLIFE VET

Dr Chloe Buiting

PANTERA
PRESS

PANTERA PRESS

The information in this book is published in good faith and for general information purposes only. Although the author and publisher believe at the time of going to press that the information is correct, they do not assume and hereby disclaim any liability to any party for any loss, damage or disruption caused by errors or omissions, whether they result from negligence, accident or any other cause. In the interests of protecting privacy, some names and other details have been changed.

First published in 2021 by Pantera Press Pty Limited
www.PanteraPress.com

Text copyright © Chloe Buiting, 2021
Chloe Buiting has asserted her moral rights to be identified as the author of this work.

Design and typography copyright © Pantera Press Pty Limited, 2021
® Pantera Press, three-slashes colophon device, and *sparking imagination, conversation & change* are registered trademarks of Pantera Press Pty Limited. Lost the Plot is a trademark of Pantera Press Pty Limited

This work is copyright, and all rights are reserved. Apart from any use permitted under copyright legislation, no part may be reproduced or transmitted in any form or by any means, nor may any other exclusive right be exercised, without the publisher's prior permission in writing. We welcome your support of the author's rights, so please only buy authorised editions.

Please send all permission queries to:
Pantera Press, P.O. Box 1989, Neutral Bay, NSW, Australia 2089
or info@PanteraPress.com

A Cataloguing-in-Publication entry for this work is available from
the National Library of Australia.

ISBN 978-1-925700-67-1 (Paperback)
ISBN 978-0-6487952-6-1 (eBook)

Cover design: Elysia Clapin
Publisher: Martin Green
Editor: John Mapps
Project editor: Anne Reilly
Proofreader: Cristina Briones
Typesetting: Kirby Jones
Author photo: Lee Knowles
Printed and bound in Australia by McPherson's Printing Group

MIX
Paper from responsible sources
FSC® C001695

The paper this book is printed on is certified against the Forest Stewardship Council® Standards. McPherson's Printing Group holds FSC® chain of custody certification SA-COC-005379. FSC® promotes environmentally responsible, socially beneficial and economically viable management of the world's forests.

*To all the nature-lovers, young and old.
This book is for you.*

All author royalties from the sales of this book will be donated to a selection of wildlife conservation organisations around the world.

For more information,
please visit panterapress.com

Contents

Prologue 1

A vet in the making

1: Lord Howe Island – paradise for a young nature-lover 7
2: Seeing ecosystems under threat 14
3: Welcome to vet school 25
4: Lola and the power of collaboration 39
5: Zoo cases and call-outs 49

Zimbabwe

6: Unexpected encounters and a very heavy 'gift' 63
7: Learning to catch animals in the wild 80

Central and southern Africa

8: Wild gorillas and chimpanzees 151
9: Malawi and a lion named Simba 175
10: South Africa 197

The Americas
11:	Central America	233
12:	USA – a far cry from Africa	247

And now?
13:	The good news stories	271

Epilogue	281
Acknowledgements	283

Prologue

WHEN A 900-KILOGRAM baby rhinoceros comes out of anaesthetic and gets cranky, you run. I was in the middle of the African bush with an enraged calf hot on my heels. On a *good* day I have the speed and agility of a tortoise. My rhino friend, on the other hand, seemed to be travelling at the speed of an Olympic sprinter. Everyone else in my team had either scaled a tree trunk, dived behind a large boulder or somehow disappeared from view. By this stage I could all but feel her breath on the back of my neck. Picturing her rather large horn, I realised I was in a fix.

The day had started normally. I was staying in a remote section of the southern Zimbabwean bush, working with the white rhino population, which is under threat. We'd been tasked with performing a complete health exam on a few of the younger rhinos in the reserve and to do this we'd been anaesthetising each animal – a safety precaution – before getting to work with our examinations. Before waking them up, we were making a small notch in the ear as part of a national monitoring scheme, so in the future we'd be able to easily identify each rhino from afar.

For close to an hour, the young rhino's mother had been waiting patiently in the distance for us to finish, hurrying us up with the occasional threat of a charge to keep us on our toes. Once the anaesthesia was reversed, the calf woke up swiftly and made – what I thought – was a beeline for her mum. What I failed to notice, however, was that as we were packing up and heading back to the truck, she turned around and was on her way to visit us once more. But rather than a quick goodbye, she seemed to have a bone to pick – and came charging at speed.

Suddenly, one of the most obscure pieces of advice I've ever received popped back into my head. 'If you're ever being chased by a rhinoceros,' a friend once told me, 'make a sharp turn to the left or the right and they won't be able to follow. Rhinos may be fast, but they aren't so good at turning.' Swiftly, I jumped to the left and watched the baby rhino fly past me, giving me just enough time to fumble my way up the closest tree.

PROLOGUE

All those years ago, as I was embarking upon my journey to become a vet, I hadn't thought I would ever find myself in a situation like that. Neither would I have pictured myself meeting elephants fitted with prosthetic legs after stepping on landmines in Asia, being at rhino-poaching hotspots in South Africa, learning to dart elephants and giraffes from helicopters, or painting eyes on cows' backsides in a truly unusual, but oddly effective, way of protecting wildlife in Zimbabwe.

So far, it's been a wild and wonderful ride. Life as a vet in the jungle is full of surprises, as you're about to find out. It's my hope that these stories will give you an insight into what's happening on the frontline of wildlife conservation. At the same time, I hope to highlight the efforts of those working tirelessly to ensure our animals are around for future generations. I'm excited to share with you my passion for this work.

A VET IN THE MAKING

1
Lord Howe Island – paradise for a young nature-lover

MY CHOICE OF career might seem logical or even inevitable. Some of my family members had been vets, and I loved animals. Trust me, though, it never felt like a foregone conclusion. And becoming a jungle vet ... well, read on and see how that all came about.

During my upbringing, I was fortunate that my curiosity about nature was fed in all kinds of exciting ways. My mum and I moved around quite a bit when I was a child, and we lived in a range of wild and exotic places. By far the most amazing of these was Australia's remote and beautiful Lord Howe Island, a tropical, crescent-shaped speck in the middle of the Pacific Ocean, where I lived from the age of eleven through to thirteen. It was covered in untouched jungle, and rich in marine life and wildlife. The population was about three hundred and there were very few cars and even fewer roads. Lord Howe was truly a tiny piece of paradise, which the great natural historian Sir David Attenborough once described as a place 'so extraordinary that it's almost unbelievable'.

Although it was only an hour or so from Sydney by plane, for the couple of years I spent on Lord Howe, it felt like I was a world away from everything else I'd previously known. I was conscious that other kids, back on the mainland, had playgrounds and sandpits; my backyard was the expansive, turquoise lagoon that wrapped around the island, and among my friends were the dolphins, sea turtles and stingrays that lived there. Immersed in nature and fascinated by the creatures around me, I added to my store of knowledge daily. It didn't take long to know what animals were friendly and those that weren't. I also learned about respect. It was essential to keep away from the captivatingly beautiful butterfly cod, with its electric red stripes and ribbon-like fins radiating out from its body. Should these fins brush against a child's body, the effects could be lethal. And, while not aggressive, butterfly cod would often be found drifting across the water, usually at the base of the rocks from where we kids loved to launch ourselves into the water. Despite needing to exercise the utmost caution – it was a prerequisite for life on the island – when I look back on those years now, I recognise that my time on Lord Howe was the start of my great love affair with our natural environment and all the creatures within it.

Like all the kids I knew on Lord Howe – and many of the adults too – I went barefoot everywhere. The morning walk to school was a scramble along the clifftops. As winter's winds were replaced by brighter days, I'd find myself weaving in and out of the palm trees and dodging diving mutton birds as they came in to land, having returned from their annual migration to Alaska. How did they do it – always arriving home on the same day every year?

School was a breeze. Well, what little time I spent there, at least. There were only about six of us in the class, all piled into a small wooden hut nestled between a stand of enormous Norfolk Island pines. Within minutes of arriving, we'd count down the hours until lunch time so we could run through the trees to the beach and jump in the water. Our favourite pastime was swimming out into the ocean, across the lagoon, racing each other to nearby 'Rabbit Island' and back – seeing who could make it the fastest, in time for the bell to ring signalling the end of our break. Other days would be spent clambering up the rocky ledges that lined the lagoon, and swinging from the vines of ancient banyan trees, using them to catapult ourselves into the glistening water below.

When I wasn't at school, I was usually exploring the jungles and cloud forests. Making my way through the endless vines and branches of the impossibly thick vegetation, I'd often marvel at the white terns. Rather than build a nest for their young, these incredible birds would lay a single egg on a tree branch and let nature do the rest. As I passed under these branches with bated breath, it concerned me that one gust of wind would knock the tiny egg off its perch and dash all hopes for the next generation. Somehow, though, it never happened. Spring would come along, the young would hatch, and you could see that, even as a tiny ball of fluff, the baby tern would be anchored to their perch by their feet and claws as if it was no trouble at all.

It never occurred to me when I was a kid just how privileged I was to call Lord Howe Island home. Because it was a World Heritage site, the island was protected from excessive development, overwhelming influxes of tourists, and most alterations to its natural state. Now I realise how rare that was. Back then it just seemed normal. If a beach had more than one other person on it, it was considered crowded. If you wanted to get somewhere, you'd have to walk or ride your bike. If the seas were too rough for the boat to deliver supplies, you'd make do with what you had. If you lived on Lord Howe, your annual calendar was based around the natural world – such as the couple of days when the tropical storms always arrived, or the events that signalled the beginning of spring.

It was spring, the time of year I loved the most, when the mutton birds returned home. All of a sudden, as if from nowhere, thousands of diving birds peppered the sky, coming in to land after a long winter abroad. Approaching at speed, they'd hurl themselves into the burrows that dotted the hilltops and I'd sit there in the paddock as they landed around me. Their natural affinity for the sky didn't extend to the land, and dodging thousands of awkwardly waddling birds became a staple of springtime. A few months later, they'd depart again, leaving their chicks in the burrows to fend for themselves as they went back north. Watching them do so was quite the event – like observing a paraglider take off from the top of a mountain. These relatives of the albatross need a big run-up before launching themselves. Once off the clifftop, they'd seem to fall towards the ground before they got enough lift to take to the sky. And then, just like that, we were left with the chicks. Thousands of them, noisily calling out from outside my bedroom for months on end before they too would eventually leave to follow their parents north.

I was every bit as fascinated by what was happening in the water, and came to love all the treasures to be found there. Gliding alongside the stingrays and reef sharks, both of which were significantly larger than my twelve-year-old self, was magic. Tropical fish of every colour would light up the ocean, and clown fish would dance in the sea anemones. I'd hold my breath and dive to the bottom of the reef, just to watch the giant clams open and close with the currents – wondering, on occasion, about accidentally being swallowed by one, given their size.

Without realising it, the outdoors became my most powerful classroom during my years on Lord Howe. Almost through my skin I absorbed knowledge about ecology and biology. Another area of interest gifted to me was conservation. Lord Howe Island was a magnet for scientists and naturalists, and from time to time teams of researchers would arrive – maybe to study rare and native species or perhaps to try to rid the island of invasive pests or predators. Naturally fascinated by their work, I spent many afternoons following them around. I was even able to tag along on various research missions, including some at sea. One unforgettable day, a group of scientists working on Ball's Pyramid, the 500-metre-high rock formation next to the island, rediscovered an ancient, alien-like insect that was believed to have been extinct since the 1920s. I felt fortunate to be living on Lord Howe Island at such a time.

These experiences fed my interest and shaped my thoughts. From my backyard, perched on a clifftop at one of the island's highest points, I could look out across the ocean at Ball's Pyramid. The remnant of an ancient volcano, it rises dramatically out of the ocean as if from nowhere. I often found myself wondering how it came to be. This curiosity extended to the ocean, where I loved to explore the coral reefs and all the creatures that inhabited them. Over the years, I observed different species come and go and watched as the coral slowly lost it colour. Back then, I had no idea about the significance of those changes and that they were related to climate change.

But most of all, in those formative years on Lord Howe Island, a seed was planted in my mind that was nurtured by all these rich experiences. It would later grow into a career that has allowed me to pursue that sense of awe and wonder in my adult life.

2
Seeing ecosystems under threat

THE CONSERVATIONISTS DAVID Attenborough and Jane Goodall were my childhood heroes. Television documentaries featuring their work helped me to develop an interest in the bigger picture. Realising that species were becoming extinct and habitats around the world were under threat, I began to consider what I could do to make a difference. I wanted to be like the scientists and researchers I'd met – to help the plants and animals and understand a lot more about how, exactly, nature works.

Why did the mutton birds return home at the same time every year? How did that egg stay on the branch despite the gale-force winds of the tropics sweeping over them?

In 2003, I left Lord Howe to attend high school on mainland Australia. Instead of dropping off to sleep to the sound of waves crashing and birds calling, I fell asleep to cars honking and passers-by calling out to one another. As I adapted to life in the city, I began to lose touch with the magic of nature. The stars were hardly visible through all of the light pollution, and I stopped looking for the Southern Cross in the night sky so I could estimate the time. And there were other details I no longer noticed – things I'd previously been fascinated by – such as the fact that you can tell east from west by the shape of a tree, or that the colour of the seeds on a palm tree can indicate what sort of winter you're about to have. I became oblivious to the subtle clues of the changing seasons, no longer found excitement in the rain arriving after a hot and dry summer, and forgot the pure joy that came from inhaling air so clean that it floods your entire body with a sense of calm. And gradually, the little things that tend to pass others by began to pass me by too.

Despite being a teenager, I never adapted all that well to the fast pace of city life and spent the vast majority of my time longing to be back in nature. Having moved so frequently as a child, one of the only constants in my life was my cat, Pep. For a kid who had been used to climbing trees and getting around an island in bare feet, the transition to city living was challenging, but if I hadn't had Pep, life would have been much more difficult. For me, growing up as an only child, he was more than a companion: we were best friends. Every afternoon after school, he'd be waiting for me at the end of the driveway, and we'd spend the weekends together in the backyard – him lazing in the sun, me poring over my homework.

Academically, I never regarded myself as gifted. But I was aware that if I worked hard enough, I'd be better able to choose the path I wanted to follow later in life. Even by this stage, I suspected that path was to become a vet. I'm sure Pep played a large role in this, even if he looked a bit different to the animals I'd hoped to work with one day. I dreamed of the animals I'd been surrounded by on Lord Howe, and of a future in which I could find myself working and living alongside them. Being well aware that this path would require decent grades, I always made sure to try my hardest in class. And, despite having a marginal aptitude for many of the subjects – particularly those like chemistry and maths that, in a cruel twist, I'd undoubtedly be needing – I somehow managed to scrape through with the necessary grades to get accepted into an undergraduate science degree at university.

Outside of school, I had a job working at the local drycleaners. It didn't pay well, but over the years that money added up, and by the end of high school in 2008, I'd saved enough to go travelling.

From the moment I'd moved to the city, I knew I wanted to escape to a place filled with nature and animals. One as far away as I could imagine. At the age of fifteen – a couple of years after leaving Lord Howe – I'd decided that place would be Africa. Early in 2009, after what felt like endless hours in the sweltering heat of that tiny shopfront, serving customers and hanging the constant stream of garments as they came out of the machine, my time finally came. Barely nineteen, I hopped on a plane and set off for the village of Muhaka on the coast of Kenya, where I'd signed on to be a volunteer at the local hospital and school.

Living in Africa proved to be every bit as magical as I'd imagined it to be. Within days of arriving in Muhaka, where I'd be based for the best part of a year, I realised that my connection to the natural world hadn't been lost as I'd feared during those years in the city. It had merely been in hibernation. Africa rekindled in me a feeling I hadn't experienced since my time on Lord Howe, one I didn't realise how much I missed until it was back.

Once more, I found myself in a remote corner of the world, surrounded by nature and wildlife. The dirt roads were studded with rocks, the ocean was a shimmering turquoise blue, and my morning commute was again spent weaving in and out of palm trees. About a hundred people lived in the village, a collection of tiny thatched huts along the roadside. Monkeys thundered across the rooftops and treetops – screaming as they went – and instead of dodging mutton birds on my way to work I'd have to sidestep the many chickens, goats and donkeys that shared the well-trodden paths through the jungle.

My confidence navigating the culture and the language, Swahili, quickly grew and soon I began to reconnect with the world I was inspired by. During my stay, I explored the local national parks and game reserves, shadowing rangers on their duties, helped out in regional wildlife hospitals and took an active role in community projects that were focused on the protection of wildlife. It was my first foray into conservation work since living on Lord Howe, and every moment I put in reaffirmed that this was the path I wanted to take in life. I spent much of my time in a remote and beautiful part of the world called Tsavo National Park, a region of central Kenya where the dirt is a vibrant red, and the landscape is so vast you can see for tens of kilometres into the distance. Here, elephants roam free by the thousands, accompanied by wandering herds of wildebeest, antelope and zebras.

Life in Tsavo could also be confronting and eye-opening. There I had my first experience observing the active destruction of the natural world and the massacre of the species that inhabit it.

Long, hot days were passed in the arid and dusty plains, tracking elephants and working with the rangers to remove snares and traps set by poachers. In this park alone, each year poachers kill thousands of elephants for their tusks, which can be sold on the black market as part of the illegal but lucrative ivory trade. Despite the numerous means at their disposal for killing the animal – from poisoned arrows to firearms and drugs – during my time in Tsavo it was becoming increasingly popular among poachers to trap the animal in a confined space. To do this, they'd dig large holes in the ground, which enticed the elephants to climb down in search of water. Once there, it was nearly impossible for the animal to get back out again, presenting the perfect opportunity for the criminals to strike.

I was staying in a small mud hut on the outskirts of the park, and every working day would start at dawn with a patrol of the grounds. Without fail, new holes would be found, and the ranger team and I would toil for days on end filling the holes back in with sticks and branches that we collected in wheelbarrows. It was challenging work, made even more so by the knowledge that this was just a small contribution to a much larger problem. For the elephant that might be spared as a result of these painstaking efforts, many others would be killed by alternative means. Poachers cleverly and quickly evolve their tactics.

Commuting between Muhaka and Tsavo was a colourful affair. I made the five-hour journey on a selection of local buses called *matatus*, which broke up the peaceful, red landscape with their strident colours and blaring music. They never really came to a complete stop to let you on board, so it was always a matter of taking a running leap into the open door as they rolled by. Then the vehicle would accelerate until it was once again tearing through the savanna, with a massive stack of precariously balanced luggage on the rooftop. A seat on one of these buses wasn't always guaranteed: often you'd have to find yourself a spot on the floor. On the occasions when I did make it on time to find myself a seat, I'd usually end up with a cage of someone's chickens resting on my lap, or next to a pig who'd also, evidently, secured themselves a ticket.

Between Tsavo and Muhaka, I was observing many echoes of life on Lord Howe. It was simpler than life in the city. Humans and wildlife lived in close proximity, and people were attuned to the comings and goings of the animals and the seasons. Again, annual routines were dictated by the weather. During the dry season, people collected reeds from the riverbanks to repair the thatched roofs of the houses, and farmers knew that the onset of the wet season was the signal for them to prepare to sow their crops.

People only took what they needed from the land and the ocean, aware that if they took any more, there'd be nothing left for the following year. They used the same approach when harvesting the reeds for thatch and to maintain the waterways. Stripping too many from the river would alter the course of the waterway and risk flooding the village in years to come.

As I watched these interactions, and people's dependence on nature in general, I came to see that the continued good health of the natural world is crucial to us all. The things I'd appreciated about nature as a child, which may have seemed whimsical, were in fact far from it. I began to learn how significant little signals from nature can be. As with appreciating art and culture, the closer you look at the natural world, the more you become aware of how interconnected we are with it. And also how dependent we are, as human beings, on a healthy ecosystem.

My time in Kenya was an incredibly formative period in which I began to understand the true importance of conservation. Daily life in Muhaka and its surrounds revolved around the ocean, and it was through this that I came to learn about the concept of 'ecoservices' – the services provided by nature that are often taken for granted. The coral reefs are a perfect example of this. They are home to a quarter of all marine life and support some of the most biodiverse ecosystems on the planet. Among a reef's marine life are organisms at the bottom of the food chain: if they die, the knock-on effect could be catastrophic. Put simply, if coral reefs are destroyed, entire marine ecosystems could collapse. Already, fish stocks are being depleted through overfishing.

But humans depend on coral reefs for more than food security: they affect people's livelihoods. It's estimated that reefs provide an annual A$30 billion worth of goods and services globally, and that one billion people are at least partly dependent on these reefs for their income. Tourism alone is a huge component of this, and in some areas of the world, entire economies depend on it.

And then there's safety. A reef is a natural barrier that absorbs the force of waves and storm surges, providing a buffer for coastal communities. According to a 2014 study published in the journal *Nature Communications*, upwards of 200 million people directly benefit from the protective effects of coral reefs. Without them we would be forced to build seawalls – an expensive, less effective and environmentally damaging solution.

In other words, if something goes wrong for the coral, then something goes wrong for each of us.

Then there's everything else a healthy natural world provides for us. Medicines are one example – many come from plants and animals, be it the venom from a cobra that's used in the treatment of leprosy, or the many lifesaving antimicrobials that we've derived from plants. We rely on insects to pollinate plants, without which we'd have no fruits, nuts or vegetables. Conserving habitats is a proven way of reducing the spread of zoonotic diseases – those shared between humans and animals. There are also the proven mental and physical benefits that come from being in nature: in Japan, this is known as 'forest bathing' and it has become a regularly prescribed therapy for people suffering from anxiety and depression. And animals can serve as indicators for environmental problems, many of which – such as the loss of peregrine falcons and bald eagles in the USA, which alerted scientists to the toxicity of DDT – would have been difficult to notice in a less diverse ecosystem.

Living in Africa was also a dose of reality – an experience that was confronting at times, particularly in Tsavo – which highlighted to me just how pressing the need for urgent action was, and still is. Our environment and all of the animals inhabiting it are facing unprecedented challenges and threats – from habitat loss, poaching, hunting, and the illegal but booming trade in wild animals for traditional medicines, meat, leather, fur and exotic pets. Many species are now facing extinction. Our insatiable demand for animal products, together with habitat loss, is driving this. And these extinctions matter. Our ecosystem is like a web in which we are all connected. There are many things capable of tearing this web apart, but one of the biggest ones is the loss of species. When extinctions happen at an accelerated rate – as they are doing right now – that web loses integrity and eventually there comes a stage where there's the potential for collapse. Humans are part of the web; we're not immune to these effects, and currently it is unravelling faster than it can be repaired. At this rate, we're charging towards a total collapse of our natural world.

Protecting the natural world was something I had to be a part of. For a long time, I'd known that my place was in the wild with the animals, just as my childhood had been. Before leaving for Africa, I'd deferred a spot at university to study science, from which I planned to progress into a veterinary degree. As my year in Kenya drew to a close, I was certain I was on the right path.

3
Welcome to vet school

I COME FROM a family of vets. I'm not talking about my mum or my dad, but the generation before them, which featured several veterinarians. Among them was my grandfather, who was a prominent equine vet in Sydney. Although I never had the chance to meet him, I grew up hearing stories about his work. Between this heritage and the conviction that my place was in the wild with the animals, attending veterinary school seemed like a logical step. But on entering vet school after finishing my science degree, any thoughts that I was about to be immersed in the world of wild and exotic animals were quickly dispelled.

The veterinary program at the University of Melbourne not only had a great reputation but was also one of the few programs, at the time, that was recognised in different corners of the world. That was extremely attractive to me because I planned to work abroad after graduation. There were only about eighty of us in the year, and within days everyone came to know each other. By the end of the first week of grappling with a timetable structured around ten-hour days – divided between the lecture theatre and the laboratory – it dawned on me that most of my waking hours over the coming few years would be spent alongside my new classmates. University was clearly going to be an all-consuming endeavour.

Lectures at this early stage were very much focused on the 'ologies' – jam-packed with just about every topic ending in such, from physiology and pharmacology to epidemiology and virology. Each day would start with around four or five hours of a selection of these subjects, followed by some sort of practical class in the afternoon. Holidays no longer existed, with weeks on end expected to be filled with 'placements', which were opportunities for us to shadow veterinarians in their everyday work. But, despite the steep learning curve and distinct lack of wildlife, I was captivated – by both the topics and the impossibly insightful professors who, over the course of the degree, were tasked with equipping us with the skills and knowledge to identify, diagnose, operate on and treat a variety of different species – no small feat.

If my conduct in many of these classes was anything to go by, the professors had their work cut out for them when it came to me.

Not only was I mistaken in thinking veterinary school would be an instant dive into the world I'd imagined for so long but I was also mistaken in assuming that my academic journey would be a resounding success. Instead, those four years were filled with monumental challenges and spectacular bungles, whereby my natural affinity for animals came into question on more than one occasion. In fact, when reminiscing on this time, there's every possibility that I have far more stories of things that didn't go to plan than those that did.

Take, for example, the bird-handling class at the beginning of first year. During what was supposed to be a relatively benign introduction to birds, a parrot latched its surprisingly sharp beak onto my finger and refused to let go. 'Make it stop!' I bellowed, at the top of my lungs, in the otherwise-silent classroom. Even now, I can picture the horrified expression on the professor's face as I frantically waved my hand and its feathery new addition about. Meanwhile my classmates found the whole thing extremely entertaining and to this day like to remind me about it.

A few months later, I built on that notoriety when a group of us were on a farm in what felt like the middle of nowhere. It was a cold day in winter, and we were bundled up in a courtyard listening to an in-depth explanation about the operations of a dairy farm. While I didn't take much away from that conversation, what I did inadvertently learn was that cows can kick in whatever direction they please, unlike horses, which can thankfully only kick forwards or backwards. In the blink of an eye, midway through an explanation on milking, a hoof very firmly made contact with my side. Later, one of my professors memorably said that a cow is able to scratch its ear with its back foot. Trust me: from first-hand experience, this means that if you're not either embracing the cow or a good three metres away from it, there's every chance you'll be sent flying across the yard.

While I'd love to report that this run-in remained the low point of my animal encounters in vet school, it was trumped about a year later when I was chased up a beach by a disgruntled and frighteningly agile sea lion in another less-than-triumphant moment of my early veterinary endeavours. Fortunately, my classmates weren't around to relish this particular failure, but *un*fortunately, a handful of bystanders were. I'd travelled to Kangaroo Island, off the coast of South Australia, to complete a placement in the summer between my second and third year of university.

It was my very first night on the island and I was sitting down by the jetty, watching the sea lions bathe on the rocks below when a passer-by expressed concern that one of the animals seemed to have sustained a deep wound. Whether it was from a boat or a shark, they weren't sure.

Recognising a chance to show off my veterinary prowess and report back to the vet clinic in the morning, I slowly edged my way down the rocks towards the enormous animal, which I could already see had a sizeable laceration running down his flank. As I got closer to inspect the extent of the injury, he suddenly turned to look at me, lifting his massive body off the rocks in a shadow of a second. The question as to *if* what I was doing was a good idea flitted across my mind, then in a flash, all 200 kilograms of him came flying up the rocks towards me with amazing agility, grace and speed for a creature that had been asleep only moments before. Quickly realising I'd significantly misread the situation (and this animal, in particular), while also coming to terms with the fact that I had to try and outrun an enraged sea lion, I managed to scramble across the terrain – thank heavens it was rocky rather than slippery – out of his way and back to safety. No doubt I gave the locals a good show in the process.

While I mentioned nothing about this to the vets in our meeting the next morning, judging by how fast news travels in small places, I'm almost certain they were treated to the colourful story not long after the fact.

By this stage I'd realised vet school was shaping up to be a steeper learning curve than I'd expected. Growing up in nature, as it turned out, was not a guaranteed recipe for success when it came to working with animals. Thankfully, most of my fellow students seemed to have met with their own fair share of challenges, and probably as a result friendships made in those first years have endured.

I'll never forget the time one of my best friends, Nikki, was sitting next to me in a lecture about reindeers. Every thirty seconds or so she'd turn and very pointedly wink at me. I didn't read much into it – she was notorious for distracting us in class, so I put it down to another of those efforts. Finally, after about twenty minutes of continuous winking, she leaned over with a perplexed look on her face. 'The joke has gone a little far, don't you think?' she whispered. When I queried what she was talking about, it turned out she'd thought reindeers were mythical creatures and that this was all for fun. Unable to contain our laughter, both of us were promptly excused from the class. (For the record, reindeers do exist.)

Each week, we had to do practicals in the laboratory. In the early years, these were a blur of pipetting one liquid into another, and hoping with every fibre of our being that the final product came out the colour it was supposed to be – signalling that the chemical reaction created had been correct. In later years, the practicals took on more of a relevant feel as we dived into topics like surgery, anaesthesia, dentistry and radiology. Having fumbled my way through the preliminary courses, I was thrilled with this new development. The days of painfully pipetting antibiotics onto agar plates to measure antibiotic sensitivities were over, replaced instead with clinical skills sessions that were designed to give us the basic proficiencies relevant to practice – from taking blood samples and placing intravenous catheters, to learning how to intubate an animal for anaesthesia and operate an anaesthetic machine, and on to scrubbing in for surgery and even acquiring some fundamental surgical techniques.

It was in the clinical skills lab that I began to see progress. The lab was a very tangible transition from student to vet and I'm sure I wasn't the only one excited about it. The room itself – despite being in a small demountable shed at the back of the university – was kitted out as if it were a hospital suite, with a selection of beeping machines, sinks, surgical gowns and equipment, and even an operating table. A selection of animal mannequins added a rather surreal touch to the room but were necessary aides in helping us practise our skills.

Of these skills, learning how to scrub in for surgery was one of my favourites, yet also one of the most challenging. In essence, it's the process of creating a sterile environment in which to operate – with the goal being to dramatically reduce the risk of infection, thereby giving the patient the best chance of a good outcome. We would line up and practise our scrubbing at the surgical sinks along the walls of the room, three or four of us at a time. Once scrubbed, the forearms must remain above the elbows, and nothing outside of the surgical field can be touched in order to maintain sterility. It's a complex and delicate task, requiring several steps to be executed perfectly in the exact prescribed order. It took great effort to remember everything that went into it, from cleaning to gowning to gloving, and this was made all the more difficult by being under the watchful eye of Anne – our small yet stern professor who ran the clinical skills laboratory with the same amount of precision and discipline that you'd expect from a drill sergeant.

I didn't know what to make of Anne at first – strict yet softly spoken, she reminded me of one of my teachers in high school, who could keep an entire class of rowdy teenagers under control by merely tapping her pencil on the desk. The difference here was that, instead making a sound with it, Anne preferred to *throw* the pencil – or anything else she could find. Rest assured, you quickly learned not to touch a thing while scrubbed and ready for surgery when she was in charge, even if that thing was flying across the room towards you. 'Maintain sterility!' I remember her repeatedly singing out, her prime objective to train us not to handle or contact anything outside of the surgical field while we were in our scrubs. Unconventional as it may have been, I have no doubt that Anne's teaching left a mark on all of us, and is in part responsible for making us the conscientious surgeons we are today. She has certainly left a lasting impression on me: there isn't a time when I scrub in that I don't think of her – and glance over my shoulder, just in case.

Of course, even in the later years there remained the odd mishap here and there. Between dodging an assortment of flying objects and doing our best to keep pace with the ever-increasing workload, there was still the occasional stumble. Like the time I confidently presented my findings on an X-ray of a dog to a class of about thirty, only to be pulled up: the patient was actually a cat, I was informed.

The exams were tough. One time, consumed by nerves, I found myself Googling 'What is an alpaca?' in a moment of blind panic the night before an exam. Still too flustered to write about them the following day, I wrote about sheep instead. In hindsight, I can only assume the 50 per cent

I was awarded for that exam was out of pity. Then again, considering we'd regularly face about twelve exams at a time – in which we'd be expected to recall every detail about any possible surgery, disease, condition or therapy under the sun – perhaps it was simply a moment of clemency.

On reflection, my biggest ever mishap occurred towards the end of the degree, at a time when I should have known better. It all started when I mistakenly allowed a friend to apply a medication to my eye to dilate the pupil so that she could practise her ophthalmic examination skills. There are two types of drugs for this – a short-acting one and a long-acting one. Unwittingly, she'd used the latter. After about half an hour, when the novelty of looking like David Bowie began to wear off, I started to get a sneaking suspicion of what had happened. It was confirmed with a quick check of the packet, and after an incredibly strained conversation with our professor on how such a scenario came to be, I left class that day with the knowledge that I'd be sitting my final exams the following week wearing an eye-patch while my pupil – and vision – slowly returned to normal.

All things considered, it might be a bit of a stretch to call my academic journey a resounding success. Still, whatever shortcomings I may have had in terms of innate ability with animals, aptitude for stress management, decision-making skills and so on, I certainly made up for in passion. Not once during the six years of university did I waver in my love for the natural world and my objective to end up in the wild with the animals I loved.

My time in Africa lingered in my mind, and I remained conscious of the fact that our natural world was under threat. A stark reminder of this came in my third year of veterinary school, when I received the news from Lord Howe that the mutton birds hadn't returned home. Rather than the tens of thousands that usually come in to land on those shores, only a handful arrived, and they were late – something they'd never been before. The ones that did arrive were scrawny and emaciated, and many died not long after arrival. It turned out that their feeding grounds in Alaska had been devoid of fish, leaving the birds to starve. The reason for this, it was later revealed, lay with the unusually warm ocean temperatures there. The krill and fish that the mutton birds normally fed on had either died or dispersed to cooler waters, leaving nothing to eat and resulting in tens of thousands of dead birds washing up on Alaskan beaches.

Those mutton birds were the canary in the coal mine – a signal that something wasn't right. That year, their failure to arrive home on Lord Howe triggered alarm among scientists and researchers, as well as among the local people who were so attuned to the comings and goings of their native wildlife that they, too, knew something was wrong. Again I was reminded that these signals from nature that may be thought of as insignificant or whimsical – whether it's noticing the colour of the seeds on a palm tree, or the number of birds returning home one year – can speak volumes about the health of our planet, if we are just willing to listen.

If the surviving birds returned to Alaska later that year, they'd do so with reduced fat and energy reserves, making them even more vulnerable to starvation. And, if the conditions were once more unfavourable for them up there, it would lead to mass deaths and perhaps even the decimation of a once-common species. The problem here, aside from the loss of a species that had as much right to be here as we humans do, is that each and every one of us is interconnected in the ecosystem. The mutton birds died because their food source in Alaska was no longer available. The food source wasn't there due to the warming oceans, and a warming ocean has far-reaching consequences for us all. One of the most notable of these is the phenomenon I was unknowingly witnessing on Lord Howe with the coral. It was losing its colour in an event known as coral bleaching – a stress response to rising sea temperatures. When the ocean temperature rises by just one or two degrees, algae called 'zooxanthellae' leave the corals, and without the algae, the coral dies. Between 2014 and 2017, around 75 per cent of the world's coral reefs experienced a bleaching event, and 30 per cent of these were severe enough to result in the death of the coral.

The problem that was first recognised on Lord Howe with the mutton birds stemmed from something that was happening tens of thousands of kilometres away – on the other side of the world, in the Northern Hemisphere. This is the ecosystem at work, and an example of how one change to the climate, to a species, or the food chain, can have far-reaching ramifications for us all.

The news from Lord Howe was a timely reminder that came as I was preparing for my final year of veterinary school. Among vet students, it's a highly anticipated time whereby you can start to pursue the direction you want to go in. The vast majority of my friends opted to follow a more traditional route, with dogs and cats. Others were keen on horses and cows. But there was no question for me: I wanted to work with the wild animals I'd fallen in love with on Lord Howe.

My time in Kenya had reaffirmed this direction. It had taught me that saving a species from extinction or a habitat from destruction is not just for the dreamers or the nature-lovers, it's something that's relevant to us all.

I'd gone there as an animal lover, believing that this is something to care about simply because we have no greater right to be here than any other species. Rather than the natural world being ours to exploit, we are its custodians – responsible for its health and longevity for both our future generations as well as those of the other species that inhabit it. But I came away from Africa certain that there is much more to it than that. Without nature, there is no us. It's the powerhouse that sustains our economy, our health and our welfare, and it's critical that we manage it correctly – not merely for its ongoing existence, but for our own.

In the summer leading up to that final year I was excited about what was to come. The students like me who were interested in pursuing this path were able to spend several months rotating through a range of zoos, learning everything we could about the animals in their care. The vision of working with elephants and gorillas and sea lions, and making a difference in the issues that mattered to me, had carried me through the rollercoaster ride of vet school so far. Now I was going to experience it for myself, hoping it would put me on a good footing to pursue a career in the wild. And, as it turned out, it would all start to come together in the most unlikely of circumstances – with a chimpanzee and a surprising plan to fix her sore knees.

4
Lola and the power of collaboration

FOR A VET aspiring to work with wildlife, anaesthesia is one of the most important skill sets to acquire. You'd be ill-advised to share a confined space with almost any wild animal when they're fully awake: it's safer for all concerned to put them temporarily to sleep before you examine and treat them.

This applies above all to chimpanzees. That's not to downplay the risks with lions and so on, but ask pretty much any zoo vet which animals would be most concerning in an escape situation and chances are chimps will be mentioned. Not only are chimpanzees highly intelligent and unimaginably strong, they also have a propensity for violence that's unseen in many other species – other than, of course, us.

Early one morning, near the end of my second month at the zoo, I was engaged in a twenty-minute battle of wits with a thirty-year-old chimpanzee named Lola, as we tried to shoot a dart loaded with anaesthetic into her. I'd had little to do with both chimps and darting at that stage. Unexpectedly, the zoo vet and I were accompanied by an orthopaedic surgeon (for humans). The two of us probably had a similar level of expertise in these matters at the time. Lola was determined not to cooperate and had no qualms about communicating her dissent. In a flurry of hissing and screaming, she hurled a pile of blankets in our direction and skilfully evaded us at every turn. We had our work cut out for us. The expression on the surgeon's face was priceless; I suspected he wasn't used to having trouble just getting his patients to sit still.

Eventually, we all made it into the examination room with Lola, now anaesthetised, and proceeded to X-ray her knees. It was clear that she was facing some challenges. Rather than the smooth white surfaces you'd expect to see on an X-ray of a normal joint, both her knees appeared irregular and crumbled. Her bone looked more like a block of Swiss cheese than a functioning knee: it was a case of severe osteoarthritis, akin to what you might see in an elderly human patient. Human arthritis sufferers describe it as an excruciating and debilitating condition.

Lola couldn't communicate directly, but her keepers had been noticing changes in her for a while. Recently, she'd stopped responding to her daily pain relief, which is often the case in the later stages of the disease.

As I looked at Lola on the table, I marvelled at the similarities between chimpanzees and humans. There's no denying our shared ancestry. In a nutshell, we are put together in the same way. From the X-rays, it would be very difficult to tell us apart, and I could almost feel Lola's pain as if it were my own. Spontaneously, I took her hand in mine and an overwhelming sense of connection flooded through me. I could have been holding the wrinkled hand of an elderly family member. When I studied her fingers, I noticed that Lola had been chewing her nails – in fact, they looked remarkably like my own fingers. I was stunned. Even this rather unsavoury habit seemed to know no species boundaries.

In that moment, I felt an intense sense of wonder that I hadn't experienced since my time on Lord Howe as a child. I was holding the hand of another thinking, feeling being. One who, in the wild, is in danger of extinction as a consequence of rampant deforestation, poaching and the illegal pet trade. Lola's family home in Africa is being destroyed due to mining for a mineral called coltan, used to manufacture mobile phones. On top of that, young chimps are being snatched from their mothers to be sold as pets. These animals once roamed far and wide, but they're becoming increasingly hard to find in the wild.

I thought, *Lola, what have we done to you?* Shame on behalf of humanity enveloped me. If we were capable of doing this to chimps, one of our closest relatives – a species that shares over 98 per cent of our DNA – what hope was there for all the other animals on the planet?

Suddenly, Lola flinched – crushing my hand in her own and startling me out of my daydream. The zoo vet had lifted her left knee and was moving it back and forth as he felt for changes within. She was still under anaesthesia, but the knee was obviously painful enough for her to react. The clicking and grinding of the bones as they moved over each other was sickeningly loud – another sign that she couldn't go on like this. Something needed to be done.

As the vet and the surgeon discussed Lola's situation, I listened intently. Although past childbearing age, she had at least ten or twenty years of life ahead of her. Time that deserved to be pain-free. Both professionals agreed that, given her otherwise good health, an intervention was necessary to help her maintain good quality of life. Had Lola been a human being, that next step would almost certainly have been a knee replacement – which is why the orthopaedic surgeon had come into the picture.

At this point, the conversation took a remarkable turn. That day, our discussion constituted the early planning stages of the world's first knee replacement on a chimpanzee! Potentially, Lola was about to make history as the inaugural patient for such a procedure. Months of planning and work would be required before such a thing could come to fruition, but being present for this conceptual stage is something I won't quickly forget. In terms of next steps, intricate CT scans – cross-sectional X-rays – of the joints would be required, from which an individual prosthesis could be made. Should it go ahead, it would require the collaboration of specialists from around the world and would be a truly monumental undertaking.

This was my first experience working in a cross-functional team, and I absolutely loved it. There's something magical about seeing the face of an eminent fifty-something professor of medicine light up at the sight of a chimpanzee or other fellow sentient being. I've interacted with obstetricians who've assisted in the delivery of gorilla babies, ophthalmologists who've helped restore sight in an elephant with cataracts, and surgeons who've been alongside veterinarians in respiratory surgeries on orangutans suffering from a cystic-fibrosis-like condition. For me, it's humbling to assist another being, and to be reminded of our similarities to other members of the animal kingdom. A reminder that we all play a role in the web of the ecosystem, and that the world does not solely belong to us.

When it comes to treating our primate cousins – with whom we share much of our anatomy, biology and behaviour – collaboration between human medical doctors and zoo and wildlife vets is not uncommon. In fact, it even has a name: One Health. The field of One Health is devoted to the philosophy that the health of humans, animals and the environment are intricately linked, and that there is much to be learned, in both directions, by veterinarians and doctors sharing their work and research.

Mammals share a highly similar genetic make-up, suffer from the same ailments and are treated in similar ways – often with the same medications. Whether the patient is a person, a dog, a dolphin, a cow or a capuchin monkey, the cellular structure is almost identical, and the diseases likely to develop – from cancer, heart disease and diabetes to depression, cataracts and arthritis – are likely to work in the same ways. This collaborative approach to medicine, and learning from species' similarities and differences, is deeply ingrained in veterinarians, who are trained to treat anything from a mouse to an elephant.

My favourite example of the benefits of collaboration between vets and doctors concerns elephants. Do you know that elephants are one of the only species on the planet that are relatively immune to cancer? Imagine the benefits if their biology turns out to hold a secret weapon to help us combat the disease in humans.

Currently, the research focus is on the so-called wonder-gene – its slightly less wondrous name is p53 (that's geneticists for you) – that's present in all mammals and is responsible for correcting errors in DNA replication within our cells. Because cancer, at its core, arises after a faulty division of cells, p53's function is critical: it corrects errors before they can manifest and also destroys any cells it is unable to fix. The fact that elephants are such large animals with so many cells would logically put them at considerable risk of cancer, given that there's so much more opportunity for error, except that they possess *twenty* copies of this p53 gene. By contrast, humans and many other mammals have just *one*.

Researchers are developing a drug that can mimic the effect of having multiple p53 genes, potentially giving us elephant-grade protection against this horrible disease.

Another angle on the potential benefits of collaboration between physicians and veterinarians is that we've now had several catastrophic global disease outbreaks – such as avian influenza, Ebola, SARS and COVID-19 – that are 'zoonotic', shared between humans and animals. Expertise from both sides of medicine is needed if control is to be successful.

Soon after we recovered Lola from her anaesthetic and returned her to the group, she let out an eardrum-rupturing scream, hurled her blanket in our direction and took off. Well, yes, the similarities between chimpanzees and humans are incredible, but the differences are still stark.

As far as the differences between working with humans and animals go, the standout is often the patient's willingness to cooperate. As I'd learned from my experience with Lola, it all starts with timing. Like us, animals have complex social structures that can be easily disrupted. This is especially true of primates.

Before getting Lola in for those X-rays, we'd spent several weeks studying her troop's dynamics to pick the most appropriate time to intervene and remove her for the examination. She was a socially low-ranking chimp, which meant there was a chance she might not be accepted back into the troop if we mismanaged that step. Because chimps tend to become quite violent, as previously mentioned, expulsion from the troop can have disastrous consequences.

Once you've chosen your moment, the next hurdle is the darting process. The challenge here is that the person who sends a projectile needle into the arm or leg of an animal as highly intelligent as a chimp – which also has a razor-sharp memory – risks being remembered as that chimp's enemy for years, even decades, to come. That means you can expect to be constantly hissed at, yelled at or spat on whenever you show your face near them, making the morning commute to work past their enclosure a colourful one to say the least. There are a couple of ways zoos get around this. One is to allocate a specific 'chimp darter' among the zoo's vets. That way, only one staffer will be on the receiving end of this behaviour and the rest will be free to have a less complicated relationship with the animals. The trouble is that this isn't much of a solution for the chosen darter.

Another option is to employ a trick commonly used by human paediatricians. Medicated lollipops, which are laced with a sedative, are often given to children prior to anaesthesia to settle them. We use the same sedative on animals, and a major benefit is that the patient often loses some memory of the events immediately *before* the sedation. This is incredibly handy if you're a vet trying to stay in a chimp's good books.

Of course, getting a chimp to eat it is a whole other matter. But if you can put the medication inside a grape or strawberry and the chimp eats the treat, you're on the home stretch.

The last hurdle in this delicate operation is to get the dart loaded with anaesthetic into the animal without being darted yourself. With chimpanzees, the likelihood of a dart flying back at you is high: often it's swiftly returned, and with surprisingly good aim, by your now-enraged target. Here, it pays to be quick on your feet if you wish to avoid both the dart and a potentially difficult conversation with your colleagues later.

5
Zoo cases and call-outs

OVER THE COURSE of that year spent in and out of different zoos, I was exposed to a variety of fascinating cases and equally fascinating patients. From fitting a penguin with a shoe to correct a foot problem and managing an angry quokka's withdrawal symptoms after finishing a course of pain medication, to caring for a female orangutan with debilitating menstrual cramps – I was enthralled with this new world of medicine. As well, I was discovering that veterinary medicine is a delicate balance of science and art. Creativity is key when working with animals, because regardless of how medically sound your plan may be, if your patient isn't on board with it – and if Lola was anything to go by, they usually aren't – you're going to run into problems. All of a sudden, you're faced with questions like, 'Will this bear eat his bandage?' and 'Can I approach that tiger to get a look at the wound?'

As for the bear and its bandages, it's safe to assume that it *will* try to eat them. Whereas popping a cone around the neck of a dog or cat usually blocks access to their dressings, that's unlikely to work with this kind of patient. Wrapping the bandages in banana leaves, on the other hand, may prevent your handiwork being washed down as the evening meal. They are not only robust – which can delay or even prevent your patient from getting to its wound – they're also rich in anti-inflammatory and wound-healing properties. Considering this, it's no wonder they've been used for centuries for wound management in human medicine. In fact, they remain popular in many countries today – so much so that some hospitals even have banana plant nurseries out the back of their burns units.

Then again, banana leaves don't deter all animals. Primates – particularly apes, which are innately curious animals – are more likely to want to pick at something than almost any other animal group. If Lola were to rip at her bandages after her knee surgery, that would be a serious concern. Luckily, while these animals are remarkably intelligent, there is a workaround: do a quick manicure with some colourful nail polish while the patient is under anaesthesia. That's often enough to distract the animal from its surgery site; it will spend the next week admiring its new manicure or picking at its nails instead. If there's no nail polish handy, other tactics include covering the animal in glue and sticking bits of paper all over them, braiding their hair so they're preoccupied with unbraiding it, or even creating 'pseudo-wounds' at other sites, with fake stitches stuck on their skin, as decoys from the true wound.

In all, I did stints in four different zoos in that final year. Each one had a different emphasis, and so by the end of the year I'd helped to treat a broad range of animals with all kinds of injuries and illnesses. Every time I thought, *It doesn't get more fascinating than this,* along would come another mind-boggling case, each one as extraordinary as the last. Take the green tree frogs with sore eyes, which had to be anaesthetised to be examined properly. Just as well frogs absorb chemicals through their skin: administering anaesthesia is simply a matter of placing them in a tub of medicated water.

When I helped take a biopsy from a hippo suffering from the skin disease vitiligo, I acquired some startling knowledge: hippo sweat is bright red! Although it looks alarmingly like blood, it's actually a special fluid packed full of a red pigment called 'hipposudoric acid' (great name – p53 geneticists take note), which acts as a natural sunscreen to protect their skin from the hot sun.

Then there was the kiwi chick – still in its egg – that, after failing to hatch, required an X-ray to determine if an intervention would be necessary. On another occasion, we ended up with a collection of paralysed pelicans, each brought in by different concerned members of the public. It wasn't down to coincidence, though. It turned out that they were all suffering from botulism poisoning. Botulinum is the paralysing toxin popularised in the beauty industry as Botox. Produced by a bacterium, this toxin can spread in waterways – often during the summer months – and waterbirds are highly likely to experience the ill effects. Fortunately for these ones, after a few days in the intensive care unit, they were able to get back on their feet.

Pelicans weren't the only birds to be brought in by concerned bystanders. Most days at that zoo, we'd treat up to a dozen wild birds, the majority of which presented with wing or feather injuries after entanglements in fishing nets or fences or run-ins with domestic pets. If left untreated, such injuries would usually be a death sentence for the animal, but these can be managed relatively simply by 'imping' – otherwise known as a feather transplant. To do this, a small bamboo skewer or thin metal wire is inserted into the cavity where the damaged feather was and is then used to secure in place the new one. We'd source these replacement feathers either from the wild, from a 'feather donor' bird or from the ever-growing number of 'feather banks' popping up to assist veterinarians with exactly this type of situation. Glue and bicarb are used to create a seal around the area, and the process is repeated for each individual feather until complete.

If that sounds fiddly, it's nothing compared to repairing a butterfly wing. Occasionally, even animals as tiny as this insect will present to the hospital. Usually, two or three of their four wings may be missing, an injury most commonly sustained from bird attacks. While many butterflies only live for a matter of days, monarch butterflies, on the other hand, can live for several months and travel over 4000 kilometres on their famous annual migration. These small but surprisingly robust animals play a critical role in the ecosystems they inhabit – pollinating jungle and forest plants along their migratory paths – and are facing increasing threats from habitat loss, notably thanks to an explosion of avocado plantations in their target destination of Mexico. For this reason, monarch butterflies can do with all the help they can get.

To reconstruct the wings of this insect, it's a matter of *cementing* on some light card – about the weight of an average business card – and extra monarch wings (one of the many peculiar things that can be found lying around a veterinary hospital) before finally dusting it over with talcum powder to prevent adhesions. Then, once the animal is warm enough to fly, it's free to go. It's one of the only surgeries I know of where the patient is able to fly off the operating table.

It's undeniable that humans have an innate fascination with the natural world, and for many, that fascination begins in the zoo. It certainly did for me. I remember being taken to the zoo as a child, even before we moved to Lord Howe Island, and becoming mesmerised by all the different animals. Twenty years on, training in zoos was every bit as enthralling. I still felt the same sense of awe when looking at Lola, or any of the other animals I came into contact with.

But zoos attract mixed responses from people, and many see them as places of captivity rather than places of sanctuary. A keystone argument for the role of zoos in our society is that people will be reluctant to protect what they don't understand. For many people, the zoo is often their first – and in many cases, only – connection to wildlife and the natural world.

Observing the reaction of visitors as they came through the gates affirmed for me the power of this connection. There is something to be said for seeing the animals yourself, learning about their plights in the wild, and perhaps even discovering ways in which you can help them, through the choices you make in your everyday life.

This wasn't the function of the zoo fifty years ago, but it is today. Zoos have become an integral part of global conservation efforts. While there is still a lot of work to be done – including addressing the fact that not every species is suited to captivity – the fact is that without the contribution of zoos, we'd be in a much more dire position than we are today.

In Australia, for example, zoos have restored populations of animals that had either been lost entirely from the wild or were soon to be. This includes the reintroduction of eastern quolls, which disappeared from the Australian mainland more than fifty years ago, and the breeding and release of southern corroboree frogs after the wild population was nearly wiped out by an infectious fungus. These may not be some of the most charismatic species you could imagine, but they're critical to the health of our ecosystems.

In America, it's the same story. Thanks to zoos, bison roam the continent once more. This iconic American species was hunted to near extinction in the nineteenth century. Because of careful breeding programs, a species whose numbers had plummeted to fewer than 500 individuals has recovered to a population of half a million and rising. The same can be said of the American alligator, which was on the verge of extinction in the 1960s. Add to the list the Mexican grey wolf, black-footed ferrets, prairie dogs, Californian condors, and the bald eagle, the very symbol of the USA. All of these are testament to the success of breeding and reintroduction programs. And with 150 species being lost on a daily basis – at least 1000 times the rate before industrialisation – these programs are critical, now more than ever.

There's also the matter of funding. Gate takings from American zoos alone fund upwards of 2500 conservation projects in more than 100 different countries, to the tune of over A$200 million annually. Without this support, which is often directed to countries where resources are limited and wildlife is under intense pressure, these projects would be unable to continue.

But perhaps the most exciting initiative to come out of the zoo world has been the recent Australian-led development of a 'poaching test'. While habitat loss remains the leading cause of extinction, poaching is hot on its heels. Most infamously, poaching has driven the rhino – an animal that has roamed the planet for the past fifty million years – to the brink of extinction in just the last decade. In fact, insidiously, the illegal animal trade has become the fourth most lucrative global crime, worth an estimated A$7 to $23 billion a year. Whether the animals are sought as pets, for traditional medicines, meat or fashion, the result is the same: hundreds of millions of animals or animal parts are being traded on the black market each year. Many are shipped alive: customs officers often find them stuffed inside boxes, suitcases, toys and appliances.

One of the biggest challenges for law enforcement is distinguishing an animal that has been illegally taken from the wild from one that has been legally bred in captivity, as many trafficked animals travel with forged documents claiming the latter. That's where this poaching test comes in. It works by picking up chemical signals through an animal's scales, quills, horns, feathers or claws – identifying not only what it has eaten, but *where* the food has come from.

The test is being developed jointly by a team from Taronga Zoo, the University of New South Wales and Australia's Nuclear Science and Technology Organisation. It was first designed by a zoo-based veterinary nutritionist in Australia. She set out to identify what echidnas eat in the wild so she could match up the diet she was formulating for their captive counterparts. The test has been further developed with the hope that it can be used by veterinary forensic specialists to help border patrol teams around the world to identify trafficked animals, return them home and prosecute those responsible.

In an ideal world, there'd be no poachers, no deforestation and no diseases transmitted by humans and our livestock. Wildlife would roam free, safe and unrestricted to do as they please. Until that time – should it ever arrive – zoos are fulfilling a critical role in ensuring the ongoing biodiversity of our planet. My time with them during this final year of veterinary school was an inspiring look into the world I'd hoped to enter for so long.

After graduating, most of my classmates intended to go into general practice. Through uni, I'd been planning to spend a year overseas working with wildlife. I'd contacted vets, hospitals, rangers, conservationists and scientists across the world, offering my services in exchange for experience. Each time someone said yes, I blocked out my diary and figured out the logistics: how to get there and what I'd need – from visas and immunisations to veterinary licensing requirements – until I had a full program, including some courses.

I was ready to move on to the conservation-focused career path I'd always wished to pursue. At vet school, I'd taken enough exams, copped enough side-swipes from cows, chased enough sheep through soaking wet paddocks and broken enough slides in the laboratory to have equipped myself with the right knowledge and skills. I wasn't yet certain in which capacity I wished to work, but I was sure that I wanted to use my career to make a contribution to the matters that were important to me.

Having grown up during the sixth mass extinction in our planet's history – Australia, shamefully, is leading the charge, with the highest rate of mammal extinction worldwide – I felt a strong calling to do my part, regardless of how small that may be.

Lola's case had had a profound effect on me and was one that would stay with me for many years to come.

ZIMBABWE

6

Unexpected encounters and a very heavy 'gift'

THE DUSTY OLD truck bumped through the Namibian desert. Keen to see a lot more of Africa, I was making my way overland to Zimbabwe via Namibia. It was January 2016 and, for the first stop on my year-long adventure, I was heading to a rural area of Zimbabwe, where I'd enrolled in a course to learn, among other things, how to dart elephants and rhinos from helicopters. Although it had only been four weeks since my graduation from vet school, I was taking notes, thinking I might write about the comically ridiculous twists and turns on the path to becoming a vet. Why not use this time on the road to start jotting down some of my thoughts and experiences? It quickly became obvious that an overland truck ride really wasn't the place to be drafting a book, so I scrapped that plan and went back to admiring the landscape out the window. My notes from the truck haven't helped me with *The Jungle Doctor*, but it's exciting to think that the seed of the idea planted all those years ago has sprouted.

What sticks in my mind about the journey north to Zimbabwe was the stifling, inescapable heat. Daytime temperatures can reach 50°C, and in the sand dunes, which punctuate the coast for hundreds of kilometres, they can easily get to 80°C. The Namibian desert is a place so dry, at least in parts, that trees which died more than 900 years ago are still standing, in perfect condition, as they're unable to rot.

It's easy to think that the landscape is barren and devoid of life, but in fact it's teeming with it. Animals such as springboks and oryx have evolved so ingeniously for desert living that they're able to thrive in such conditions, requiring little or no drinking water to survive. As for the insects and reptiles, they take shelter in the depths of the sand during the day and come out at night to collect what little moisture they can from the evening sea breeze.

Namibia's answer to Uluru in Australia or Monument Valley in the USA is a place called Spitzkoppe, and I fell in love with it. Dotting the breathtaking desert plains of cacti and scrub are towering structures of enormous red boulders. These boulders have been smoothed and shaped by rainfall over millions of years, and if you climb to the top of them you'll find large pools eroded into the rock face, providing a perfect spot to cool off in the heat. I remember sleeping under a sky impossibly full of stars, drifting off to the sound of zebras snorting and oryx clanging horns, and waking in the morning to find jackal tracks scattered around the sleeping mats. The locals liked to insist that the real magic of the desert came in the mornings, when making the coffee was simply a matter of sitting the jug of water on the sunny side of the dune for half an hour or so.

Further north, the red sand of Namibia quickly gave way to lush, green foliage as I crossed into Botswana. Flooded with about three trillion tonnes of water each year from Angola, Botswana's famous Okavango Delta swells into a lush paradise that's home to a diverse and highly concentrated population of wildlife. It also happens to be home to a subtropical species of plant with thorns so large that if you accidentally step on one, it can easily pierce any material – to semi-permanently attach your foot to your shoe, for example. This is, unfortunately, something I learned the hard way.

It was a relief to finally arrive in Zimbabwe, by which time I'd thankfully managed to remove my foot's new appendage. I'd planned to spend just over a week in the small but bustling town of Victoria Falls before heading out into the Zimbabwean bush for the course. While I was very much looking forward to it, I had hardly any idea of what I'd signed up for.

To pass the time in Victoria Falls, I'd decided to pay a visit to one of the local vet clinics, which was located a little out of town. Apparently, the walk there entailed dodging wayward elephants, which I didn't quite fancy. Luckily, one of my new friends in town had a motorbike and agreed to take me. He turned up at my accommodation at seven in the morning, grinning from ear to ear and proudly clutching a bag of *mabhanzi* – a traditional Zimbabwean sweet bread – for me to snack along the way. As I ran out the door, I grabbed a scrub top and threw it in my bag on the off chance I'd be allowed to shadow the vet at work.

After about twenty minutes of rocketing through the dusty backroads of Victoria Falls on my guide's beaten-up but well-loved bike, we arrived at the clinic. It was a small brick building at the end of a long and winding road, sitting on top of a hill. Below lay bright green jungle; above, monkeys were howling in the trees; warthogs were grazing on the surrounding vegetation. It was one of the most picturesque locations for a veterinary clinic I'd ever seen. Immediately, it conjured up thoughts of the movie *The Lion King*, which I'd loved as a child.

Inside, I was greeted by the owner of the practice, Dr Gordin Moyo, who enthusiastically rushed to shake my hand. He wasted no time in giving me a comprehensive tour of the place, and introduced me to all of his staff. The practice had two vets, including him, a receptionist and a nurse, who was a young man who'd just left school. It was apparent how much Gordin adored the animals in his care, and to this day I've never seen anyone as gentle or compassionate with even the most aggressive or mange-riddled dog.

The clinic was modest, and consisted of a consultation room, a surgery, an office and an overnight room for the vet on call. Out the back were some kennels with palm-thatched roofs, and a concrete plunge pool where the animals could be bathed in anti-parasitic medication. They also had a small compounding pharmacy on site where they made many of their own medications to help make veterinary treatment more affordable for the community. Gordin explained the general day-to-day happenings in his clinic, which saw about ten to twenty patients a day. Most of these were pets and livestock, but he also tended to a lot of wildlife, including many with aggression issues (but we'll get to that later).

After the tour, I think something might have got lost in the excitement of the morning as I was promptly handed a white coat and a stethoscope and guided into the adjacent consultation room. When I turned to see if my mentor was behind me, I was instead met by a woman who wasted no time in plonking her new puppy down on the examination table and launching into its long list of ailments.

After excusing myself, I rushed from the room to clear up this misunderstanding. Even if I'd had a licence to practise in Zimbabwe – which I didn't – I certainly wouldn't have imagined my first consultation going this way. Like any new graduate, I was pretty unsure of what I was doing at the *best* of times, let alone while on the other side of the world, communicating in broken English, and with mere seconds to prepare. Thankfully, after a brief discussion, Gordin and I swapped lab coats (he took white and I took blue) and we went back into the room together. Later, I found out that blue signalled the colour of an assistant, and that's what I became for the rest of my time there.

Over the following handful of days, I turned up at the clinic promptly at eight o'clock. Tearing along the bumpy dirt roads of the towns and villages of rural Zimbabwe on the back of a motorbike remains one of the most fun ways

I've ever got to work. By contrast, back home in Melbourne the following year, driving the Nepean Highway each morning was the biggest drag of my life.

Days here were largely divided between appointments in the clinic and house calls in the village, and it wasn't long before I started to think that I should have paid more attention in my second- and third-year bacteriology, virology and parasitology classes. Every second dog seemed to be suffering from some exotic disease with an equally exotic name. Many of them were also suffering from canine distemper virus, which made me think of my grandfather, who was a practising vet in Australia in the 1950s, '60s and '70s when this devastating disease was rampant. In recent decades, thanks to the availability of a distemper vaccine, cases of the disease have become few and far between in Australia, although worryingly, vaccination rates have begun to fall. In Zimbabwe, the vaccine is far less available, and consequently it's no surprise that my very first run-in with this horrible disease was here.

My professors at university said that once you've seen a case of distemper, you'll never forget it. They were right. The dogs present shaking, twitching and falling over, with a horrible, thick discharge coming from their nose and eyes. At best, an afflicted animal has an extremely poor chance of survival, and it's a truly awful thing to treat.

Once thought to primarily infect dogs, the virus has now also begun to wreak havoc in populations of unrelated species in the wild. From lions in the Serengeti to giant pandas in China, the virus has adapted and mutated, causing devastation in animals that are already facing enormous challenges from poaching, hunting and habitat loss. The spread is thought to have been facilitated, at least partially, by the increasingly close proximity in which we – and our pets – live with wildlife, and drastic measures to control it have begun. In China, large-scale vaccination programs of pandas are underway, and the same is being discussed in Tanzania for the lions.

Out of the clinic and between house calls, we'd spend the afternoons in the local game reserves tending to some of the larger patients. It was the time of the year when the local elephants were starting to cause trouble, and it was the vets' responsibility to put in place measures to keep the community safe.

Unbeknown to many people, including me at that stage, about once a year, adult male elephants enter a period called musth, where their testosterone levels skyrocket and their behaviour changes. Although, having since witnessed it first-hand, calling this a behavioural 'change' may actually be a bit of an understatement. I'll rephrase: musth is a time when a perfectly placid bull elephant can morph into a deranged, Hulk-like beast. More volatile than a pubescent teenager, an elephant in musth is likely to go on testosterone-fuelled rampages, resulting in mass destruction and havoc for the surrounding towns and people. An elephant in musth is capable of trampling villages, attacking people and picking violent fights with rhinoceroses. The rhinos usually come off second best in such encounters, and the same can be said of people.

This is one of the many challenges that comes part-and-parcel with living in close proximity to wild animals. Admittedly, the problem gets acutely pressing if the animal in question happens to be an elephant with poor anger management. In these instances, human safety is a primary concern, and there are several tactics that can be used to keep the elephant's aggression under control. A common method – which we used here – is to vaccinate a problem animal with a hormone-suppressing drug. By doing this, the levels of testosterone are reduced to 'regular' levels, and the associated behaviour abates. Another method is to introduce a bigger, older bull into the group. Within a matter of days, the younger and smaller elephants will have come back into line.

In this instance, the conflict is very much one-sided – the elephant is picking the fight. In many others, however, the conflict goes both ways. Farmers and locals have to contend with elephants trampling their crops and lions eating their livestock, which, in both scenarios, will usually mean that the person's entire livelihood is at stake. Naturally, the farmers retaliate. When that happens, you get outcomes such as animals with spear wounds, trapped in snares, shot and even poisoned, all of which I've seen. This is the core of what's known as human–wildlife conflict, an enormous and ever-growing problem on the African continent. It's a no-win situation, with neither party truly at fault.

With this in mind, I used my last few days in Victoria Falls to go into the local National Parks office, which was closely associated with a small but active Anti-Poaching Unit. I'd heard about some work being done to combat the human–wildlife conflict here in Zimbabwe, including some creative and unconventional methods using bees, paint and flashing lights, which I was eager to see for myself.

On arrival, the place was swarming with people. They'd just apprehended a huge load of ivory that was being smuggled across the Zambian border into Zimbabwe. In some countries, the law says that this stockpile is to be destroyed by incineration, but here in Zimbabwe it would be stored in a safe location instead. I waited for the commotion to die down before introducing myself to the officer at the front desk, and was directed to a ranger in charge of the community outreach programs. By default, he was also leading the resolution initiatives when it came to matters of human–wildlife conflict. He wasted no time in taking me in and enthusiastically explaining the projects they were currently working on. By chance, he was heading out to a farm that afternoon. What had prompted the visit, he explained, was a call he'd received a few days prior from a farmer who'd been having trouble protecting his livestock from lions. The ranger, along with a local researcher, had arranged for a group of schoolchildren to meet him out there to assist with the project while also learning, firsthand, about human–wildlife conflict.

We proceeded to load up the car with several tins of black paint and a fistful of paintbrushes – which at the time I remember thinking wasn't much of a match against a hungry lion – and set off into the bush. On the way we stopped at another farm, which had several large boxes on sticks around its perimeter. The boxes had small thatched roofs, were spaced about 10 metres apart from each other, and had a thin wire running between them. On closer inspection, they were beehives, and what I was looking at was a beehive fence. The ranger explained how some research by zoologist Dr Lucy King from the Save the Elephants Foundation in Kenya had turned up the unexpected finding that elephants were terrified of bees. This was something that could easily be used to the farmers' advantage. When I say terrified, I mean that at a mere *buzz*, a 5-tonne, fully grown elephant is likely to turn and sprint off into the distance, trumpeting as they go. When these boxes are placed around a farm, the sound of the bees is often enough to deter any elephant considering trampling the enclosed land. In the cases where the sound *isn't* enough to send the elephant running, the small wire connecting the boxes releases all of the bees from their hives upon impact, and that's certainly guaranteed to do the trick!

I hopped back into the car, stunned that something as small as a bee could be enough to protect an entire farm from a stampeding elephant, and marvelled at how simple a solution the idea of the fence was. As we drove on to the farmer who was having problems with predators taking his livestock, I'd soon be seeing another effective, non-violent solution to a serious problem.

As we approached the driveway of the second farm, the ranger told me that ongoing drought in Zimbabwe had meant that lions, which normally preferred to stay away from communities, had been forced closer and closer to settlements in search of food. One of the most readily available food sources here was, of course, livestock, and as a result, conflict between humans and lions had been escalating out of control.

In some places, the problem was being tackled by applying other interesting research findings: this time, that lions are acutely averse to flashing lights. There were pilot programs underway whereby lights were installed around farms to protect the animals. But not all farmers were able to afford such a thing – and that is where our tins of paint came into the picture.

About twenty excited schoolchildren ran alongside the car all the way up to the small, wooden hut where the farmer lived. Out here, the devastating effects of the drought were obvious immediately. There was a complete lack of vegetation on the ground; dust billowed in every direction; there was a shimmer on the horizon from the oppressive heat; and the livestock clearly had had very little to eat for months on end. These were dire times for many people who depended on the land for their livelihoods, a situation compounded by predator attacks on their livestock.

We unloaded the paint, and the ranger gathered the children to explain the issue and what we'd be doing to combat it in a way that didn't involve violence. It was vital to educate these children from a young age about the problems facing their society, and to raise the next generation with the skills and knowledge of non-violent solutions to ensure future harmony between the people and wildlife of Zimbabwe. Not only was this important from a human *and* animal welfare perspective, but it was also important for tourism, given that so much of the country's economy relied on visitors coming to go on safari and see the local wildlife.

Thanks to the excitement and hubbub, I only caught about every third word of the ranger's explanation, but I got the gist, and my surprise at a fence of beehives was quickly replaced by total disbelief about what we were about to do. Initially, I suspected that he was having a joke with the children (or potentially with me), but when the farmer started to gather his herd, it was obvious that this was no laughing matter. Our task would be to use the black paint to draw eyes on the backside of each cow, one on either side of the tail, in what can only be described as the most unusual afternoon of my life to date. While this was my first encounter with this truly astonishing technique to keep hungry predators at bay, it is actually a tactic with a firm grounding in science, and one that is used in many parts of the world.

Research conducted by Dr Neil Jordan, a conservation biologist at the Taronga Conservation Society Australia, suggests that by painting two eyes on a cow's rear-end, you 'trick' a potential attacker into thinking it's being watched, intimidating the animal and preventing it from hunting the cow. As is usually the case, nature is several steps ahead of us, and there are multiple examples of this exact same trick throughout the natural world. Butterflies, insects, reptiles, birds, fish and even some cats exhibit natural eye markings, also known as 'eyespots', on their wings, coats and scales to reduce their chances of being eaten as prey. But it's not just the animals that use eyespots. For centuries, people living and working in the jungles of Asia have fashioned masks that look like faces and worn them on the back of their head as a form of protection against tiger attacks, although I'm not sure how I'd feel about a flimsy piece of paper being all that's standing between me and a large peckish cat!

Initial disbelief aside, I had to admit that the science was there and, given that the local lion population in Zimbabwe had dropped by close to 90 per cent in the past forty years, anything was worth a try. If it worked, everyone stood a chance of benefiting – the farmers could keep their livestock and therefore their income, the cattle could avoid becoming someone's evening meal, and the lions would be spared from the farmer's retaliation. So, without hesitation, we divvied up the cows between us and got to work as Zimbabwe's new Picassos. Coincidently, that's not too far off what the cows looked like just a few hours later!

Once all of the cows were sporting new artwork on their backsides, the ranger, researcher and I drove back into town. It had been a long, hot and dry afternoon out in the Zimbabwean sun and part of me wondered whether I'd become delirious with sunstroke and imagined the entire thing.

I got back to my hotel room exhausted from the week, but I didn't want to waste my last evening in this beautiful town, so I made my way to the banks of the massive Zambezi River to watch the sun go down. There I was, surrounded by bush at the top of the awe-inspiring Victoria Falls, watching the mist from the falls rise and the sun set while the water rushed past, roaring as it cascaded off the rocky edge in the distance.

The sky was darkening when I decided to make a move; I didn't want to risk a run-in with a dusk-dwelling animal. But I'd left it too late. Halfway home, I came face to face with an adult bull elephant that popped out from the frangipani trees right in front of me. In my head, I was already bolting down the road, but in reality, my feet seemed to be firmly glued to the ground. It was just as well, given that only days beforehand I'd learned about the futility of trying to outrun an upset elephant. My thoughts jumped to the hormone injections from earlier in the week, and I hoped like crazy he'd had his. As I watched, frozen to the spot, this behemoth flapped his ears and retreated silently back into the scrub.

Early the next day I was standing outside in the cool morning air, waiting for my taxi to the airport, when my friend with the motorbike came past to say goodbye. As was our routine for most mornings this week, he'd brought me a bag of *mabhanzi* to eat along the way, but this time he carried a second bag that looked – and felt – suspiciously like it contained a tonne of bricks. When I looked inside, I gulped. It wasn't exactly bricks, but it may as well have been. The bag was full of perfectly round, smooth light-grey rocks that were about half the size of the palm of your hand. He'd mentioned something the other day about these unusual rocks on the banks of the river, which had turned up in recent years in the thousands. In hindsight, I wish I'd simply nodded. Instead, I made the mistake of saying that some members of my family were avid geologists who'd surely be able to tell him what they were. Thanks to this passing comment, I was now the recipient of no fewer than eighteen deceptively heavy Zimbabwean stones. Surely my friend didn't expect me to bring them with me through Africa and the Americas, then home to the geologist in question! Yet I couldn't bring myself to refuse them. So, into my bag they went and, after a heartfelt goodbye and the promise that I'd be back to Victoria Falls one day, my new collection of rocks and I headed to the airport.

7
Learning to catch animals in the wild

PRIMARILY, I'D COME to Zimbabwe to undertake advanced training in wildlife capture and anaesthesia. This is both a highly specialised field and a critical part of every wildlife veterinarian's work. The mere term 'capture', I found, would evoke confusion and bewilderment among my friends and family (who still, at the best of times, have little idea of what I do), so I started instead telling them I'd be learning how to 'catch wild animals' – even though that's really a bit of a stretch.

On the short flight from Victoria Falls to Harare, the capital city of Zimbabwe, I frantically scanned as many research papers on the topic of wildlife anaesthesia as I could. Before leaving Australia, I'd downloaded a bunch of them onto my tablet, although I suspected this wouldn't make much difference to what was sure to be my gross incompetence on the course.

On the off chance that any of those aforementioned family members are reading this book, perhaps now is a good time to provide a more adequate explanation of what, exactly, wildlife capture is. (My aim is to prevent anyone picturing me sprinting through the African bush and launching myself onto an unsuspecting zebra.) In essence, wildlife capture is the practice of using medical or physical techniques to restrain or immobilise a wild animal for treatment or translocation. In practice, it's about using drugs, darts, ropes, nets or a combination thereof, to bring an animal into a situation where you're able to handle it safely.

The capture is almost always done for one of two reasons: either to enable you, as a vet, to treat the animal, or to move it from one place to another. In the case of treatment, some people may question why a wild animal needs to be treated at all. The species has survived in nature, perfectly capably, for millions of years, so what would warrant human interference in this? Well, while it's a reasonable question, most often the answer comes straight back to us. It's exactly *because* of human interference that treatment becomes necessary. Many of these instances involve wild animals caught in snares or wire traps by hungry locals wanting bush meat, hunters looking for prey, or disgruntled farmers protecting crops or livestock. In particularly horrific cases, the animal in need of assistance may be a rhino left for dead by poachers who've brutally hacked off its horn for trade on the black market, or an elephant that's been viciously debilitated so people can harvest its tusks. Perhaps even more devastatingly, it may even be a calf of one of these two species, left alone after its mother has been killed, and, unless there was intervention, destined for a slow death from starvation and dehydration.

Of course, there are rare instances where we are *not* directly implicated in the animal's suffering. These may include disease outbreaks and natural disasters, which, in both cases, still require management to ensure the animal's welfare is maintained. For disease outbreaks, an animal may be captured so we can take a sample of blood to monitor the spread and progression of the disease – especially if it poses a threat to additional species, or even to human life. We may also need to put a collar or monitoring device on the animal to track its movements, which is especially important in scenarios where they roam in close proximity to people.

The same question, or perhaps even concern, can be asked about translocation. Why on earth would you want to intervene in a wild animal's life so drastically that you have to physically move it from one place to the next? Again, the answer usually finds its way back to us. The truth is that we've interfered so heavily in wild habitats, notably in Africa, that very few places are truly wild anymore. Factors such as encroaching townships or the large fences around national parks mean that the natural movements of animals have been restricted, and so these ecosystems now require active management.

Problems like the overpopulation of one species and the subsequent decimation of a certain food source may mean that individual animals, or entire herds, need to be relocated to a different region to allow the survival of both themselves and the other species that share this habitat. Alternatively, in these enclosed systems, dwindling numbers of animals – for whatever reason – may lead to reduced genetic diversity of the species, necessitating the introduction of new animals to ensure their survival in that area. Even something as straightforward as drought in a particular region, such as the devastation that Zimbabwe was (and still is) facing at this time, may make an area uninhabitable for both humans and animals alike, requiring the removal of these herds to – literally – greener pastures.

On a more sinister note, animals may also need to be moved because of the threat of poaching, which is more prevalent in some countries – and specific regions within those countries – than it is in others. Many factors play into why these areas are poaching 'hotspots', such as local law and governance, penalties for acts of poaching, socioeconomic pressures, demand for certain products, and the ease of access to the animals. South Africa's famous Kruger National Park is one of these notorious hotspots, as is the region of Zimbabwe I'd just arrived in. In these places, as drastic as it may sound, many of the species that are under extreme threat of poaching are being moved out of the region and into neighbouring countries where their safety can be more assured.

Rhinos, especially, are being walked, driven, slung from helicopters and even flown in military aircraft to get them out of harm's way in a situation that's become so dire it can only be described as a war zone. The veterinarians who accompany them, as I was soon to find out, are escorted by armed guards to ensure both their safety and that of the animals. Poachers have become so desperate that they'll stop at nothing to retrieve their bounty. In fact, for species with targets on their heads, the threat of poaching has become the number one reason for their capture and translocation. Nowadays, that's even an industry in itself, and to keep up with the demand there are full-time veterinarians employed.

A little clearer about what wildlife capture is – or, more specifically, why it's necessary – I was ready to learn how it's done. I'd come to Zimbabwe to be trained in how to handle, dart, treat and move these animals, desperately wanting to do what I could to help; I could no longer remain passive. Should everything go well over the next fortnight, I'd be leaving with the capability to do exactly that – provided I passed the extremely difficult, day-long exam at the end of the course.

It was almost a year to the day since I'd signed up for it, and now here I was, in the middle of Harare airport, wondering what on earth I was going to do next. I hauled my backpack off the conveyor belt at the luggage collection, cursing the stones as I did, and made my way outside into the chaos of hundreds of eagerly awaiting taxi drivers. I'd accidentally booked myself on the incorrect flight, which meant that rather than being collected with several of the other course attendees, I'd need to make my own way to the meeting point. Luckily, as is common at airports – and this one especially – I had my pick of drivers willing to assist, and it took me no more than a minute to find someone who knew exactly where it was I needed to go.

Coming from the quiet town of Victoria Falls, I found it overwhelming to be back in a big city. Harare is a sprawling, chaotic and bustling metropolis where there are seemingly few road rules, and certainly even fewer that are abided by. Leaving the airport, we skidded through narrow alleyways, dodging cows, chickens and pigs as we went, and shot out the other side into a maze of six-lane freeways. At least the apparent lack of road rules or etiquette made for a quick trip, and within about fifteen minutes of watching the city flash by us, we were pulling up outside a small bed and breakfast. According to the welcome booklet I'd been sent several months prior, this was the designated meeting place, and where we'd be staying overnight as a group before setting off into the bush in the morning.

The accommodation wasn't exactly what I'd imagined as I was booking the course. It was completely enclosed in 6-metre-high, cold, concrete walls, topped with thick coils of barbed wire, which looped their way around the perimeter. The gate was a solid metal sheet, revealing nothing of what lay inside. I was beginning to get an inkling that security was a priority around here, judging by how seriously residents in the surrounding neighbourhoods appeared to take it as we passed through.

My nerves tingling, I stepped out of the taxi and approached the guard at the front gate, only to find that this completely abated when I was greeted by name and warmly welcomed inside. To my surprise, the gates opened into a lush, green jungle of a courtyard that could only be described as an inner-city oasis. It was humming with myriad bird calls, and for a moment it was hard to believe where I was standing, given my initial impression only seconds before. Looking around, there were about twenty small cabins that lined the courtyard, and presumably one of them was mine. As I made my way to the check-in area, I heard my name being called out by a group of about ten people who were sitting around a barbeque in the middle of the lawn. They were my course mates, I realised. Having managed to book the correct flight, they'd made it here several hours before me. Someone handed me a cold local beer (appropriately named Lion Lager), and I plonked down my backpack so I could join them on the grass.

As it turned out, I wasn't the last to arrive. About fifteen more people wandered in after me, and within the hour, all twenty-five of us were gathered around the barbeque as it was being fired up for dinner. We spent the evening relaxing in the courtyard and getting to know each other, and it didn't take me long to realise that I was among some of the most accomplished and remarkable people I'd ever met. Because I'd spent my entire six years of university suspecting I was the slowest person in the room (impostor syndrome), I was no stranger to these feelings of inadequacy. The difference between vet school and my current situation, however, was that I was almost certainly the class dummy this time. There we were, a group of (mostly) veterinarians and conservationists, hailing from different corners of the world, working in a range of different capacities and roles. Everyone I spoke to seemed to have an incredible story about their experiences and contributions to the field of wildlife conservation, and there I was, fresh out of university. Yet I wasn't complaining; I felt privileged to be in the company of such people, many of whom have since become good friends and colleagues.

One of the first people I hit it off with, probably because he was the guy who handed me the beer, was a vet from France who was several years ahead of me, and remarkably accomplished given his stage of career. After graduation, he'd completed an internship – much like the punishing year that was lined up at home for me in Australia – and had then moved to Zambia to set up an elephant hospital where he now worked. Joining the conversation was a woman from Germany who'd just moved to South Africa to complete a PhD in rhino genetics, and who was actively involved in developing a genetic test to link a poached rhino horn to the carcass from which it came – changing the game for the prosecution of those involved in such activity. Then, of course, there were local wildlife vets who hailed from different parts of Africa and worked with a spectacular variety of species. I was particularly moved to meet a veterinarian who puts his life on the line to protect gorillas in the depths of wartorn Congo. He was attending this course to renew both his skills and licence to dart and transport these animals from regions of conflict to areas of heightened security. Similarly, there was another veterinarian, who quickly became a good friend; he led an annual project that flew rhinos from South Africa to Botswana in an effort to ensure their safety in the midst of the poaching crisis. As it turned out, he worked on this project with Prince Harry, who is well known for his passion for conservation, and it was a surreal experience to see my friend on the television at Harry and Meghan's wedding in London a couple of years later.

If this evening was anything to go by, it was going to be a transformative two weeks in the Zimbabwean bush. Some of us, like me, had come as novices, hoping to gain the skills and knowledge necessary to participate in this line of work. The veterans, on the other hand, had been in this field for decades and had come to renew their licences in order to carry on their work, which they had to do roughly every five years – depending on where they were based. Somehow, though, whatever our level of experience, we'd gathered here as students and colleagues, and I think we all shared the same excitement about what was to come – regardless of whether it was our first time here, or our tenth. The reputation of the course preceded it, and I was beginning to get an inkling that it was going to be a fortnight to remember.

Eventually, we peeled ourselves away from the barbeque at around ten that evening and went to our cabins. I never did end up checking in, but the entire facility had been reserved for us, so I picked the closest empty room and stumbled into it, ready for bed. The next thing I registered was the alarm sounding; somehow it was already six in the morning. When I peeked through the curtains, I saw that six four-wheel drive vehicles were waiting for us in the courtyard. Half the group was already there. Once again, I was running late. After fumbling my way into some clothes and hurling my few belongings into my backpack, I sprinted out the door.

I reached the cars only to find that we still had an hour left before departure, but was so flooded with adrenaline by that stage I decided to deposit myself right there and await further instructions. The plan, I gathered, was to split into six groups and convoy our way out of Harare to our destination, seven hours deep into the bush. Each group was to be supplied with a map. Hearing that, I couldn't help feeling I was now somewhere between a schoolkid on camp doing an orienteering exercise and a participant in *The Amazing Race*. Nevertheless, once the rest of the group arrived, we dutifully loaded ourselves into the vehicles and set off for whatever this next adventure would bring.

The landscape changed dramatically as we left the city behind, and before I knew it, I was seeing a side to Zimbabwe I'd never seen before. The vegetation was thick and green, the hills became mountains and the landscape was littered, just like in Namibia, with giant red boulders. The bitumen roads of the city and townships morphed into a dirt track that became progressively bumpier as we went. Wildlife was everywhere – giraffe heads peering through the treetops, monkeys running wild and zebras lazily grazing along the roadside.

We crossed dried riverbeds with near-vertical walls that were even a challenge for our heavy-duty vehicles to traverse, and got to a stage where we were driving through nothing but tall grass. We'd left all semblance of a road or path hours behind us, and inevitably, with practically no road signs or even the vaguest indication of where we might be, we came to the conclusion that we were lost. And also almost certainly mere hours away from becoming a lion's evening meal. My mind drifted back to the cows and the painted-on eyes, and I briefly wondered if I'd soon be in a desperate enough position to give it a go myself.

Fortunately, the returning attendees of the course managed to redirect us, and sometime in the early afternoon we pulled into the long, baobab-lined driveway of the game reserve that was to become home for the next fourteen days.

Baobab trees are, to me, one of the most iconic African sights I could imagine, and it's no wonder they are known here as the tree of life. Not only are they imposingly tall, commanding attention from kilometres away, but their thick and solid trunks act as a water source for people and animals in times of drought. These trunks begin to hollow as the tree ages and can then be used as a place for ceremonies, shelter or even housing. They are simply ancient trees – living for thousands of years – making it a humbling and awe-inspiring experience to be in their presence.

The driveway itself was actually more of a dirt path, winding between boulders and cliff faces, and speckled with the tracks of the lions, wild dogs, elephants, rhinos and antelope that call this place home. It was truly the wilderness, a place so remote that you could easily think you were the only person on earth, and light-years away from any form of civilisation. Eventually, we pulled into the camp. It was in a small clearing of the bush encircled by a wooden fence, which was a necessity to keep out the four-legged neighbours. We unloaded the cars and walked through the gate, to be met with a scene not too dissimilar to the one from the previous day. Unexpectedly, it was a lush jungle in here, an ecosystem unto its own, all centred around an enormous baobab tree with sprawling branches and hanging vines swinging in the afternoon breeze. In the middle of the camp was an open-air dining area with a small adjacent kitchen. Long communal dining tables had been set up for our dinner, a surprisingly elegant sight in our bush surroundings. Small thatched-roof huts (known as bomas) were arranged around the edge of the camp, and towards the back was another open-air building, presumably a classroom or lecture theatre.

Under the tree, waiting to greet us at a welcome table, were the course instructors, who also happened to be some of the best known and most accomplished wildlife veterinarians in the world. These were authors of my textbooks in university, people I'd read about and idolised in school, and meeting them was an unsurpassable experience. They welcomed us to the course, checked us into the program one by one, and gave us each a bag. It struck me that this bag of course materials weighed as much as my backpack with gear for the entire year, including the several kilos of stones. The enormous, printed and bound lecture book was almost thicker and heavier than the one I'd compiled for my final exams at university. There was also a textbook on the topic of wildlife capture and a handful of laminated charts that I'd sort through later. At the bottom of the bag, however, was a colourful tag that caught my eye. It bore the word 'Giraffe'. When I glanced across to my friend, the French vet from Zambia, his tag had the word 'Rhino' on it. These were of great significance: we'd been allocated to one of four groups – giraffe, rhino, lion and elephant – according to which species we'd be directly involved in capturing.

I was in for a thrilling and physically challenging time. Giraffe capture is one of the most demanding wildlife immobilisations of them all. Finding that out, however, was ahead of me. For now, I was simply feeling dazzled.

The theory

That evening, after a welcome dinner and introductory session where we got to know one another, including the instructors, we made our way to our allocated rooms. Half the group would be staying here, in the small bomas around the site, and the other half would be in a second camp about a ten-minute drive away. Everyone had been given a roommate, and mine was Fidu, a vet about my age from the Austrian province of South Tyrol, who was intent on moving to South Africa to become a rhino vet (a goal she'd later achieve). Fidu and I had been put in a boma in the second camp, so along with the rest of our group we took our luggage over to the old safari utes waiting for us at the entrance and jumped on board.

It was February, the tail-end of summer, when the sun sets late in that part of the world. Despite it being nearly ten at night, it was only just the beginning of dusk. It gave the drive a special quality that is hard to put into words. It wasn't a one-off because that drive back to camp proved to be one of the most magical parts of every following day, too. Riding in the tray of the truck as it bumped its way through the ancient baobab and acacia trees, the warm air blowing in my face, under a black sky lit up with stars, is a memory I'll never forget. The enormous overhanging branches along the track were silhouetted against the night sky, and it wasn't unusual to see a leopard or two reclining among the leaves. We'd pass lions, wild dogs, zebras and rhinos on these drives, all of whom seemed completely unfazed by our presence. On occasion, we'd even see the odd impala, which, just like the kangaroos back home, would always try to throw themselves in front of the headlights, making extreme caution necessary.

It was on this first night that I received my first true lesson of the bush. As we came around a corner we found ourselves within touching distance of a silently ambling elephant. He stopped in his tracks as abruptly as we stopped in ours. We looked at each other, neither party making a move until, suddenly, he raised his trunk and let out an earth-shatteringly loud trumpet. In my spot on the tray of the truck, not only was I so close to him that I could see every wrinkle on his body as he towered over us, but I could also feel my teeth rattle in their sockets as his call reverberated through the air. He began flapping his ears menacingly and took two deliberate steps towards us, whereupon my heart froze and I momentarily forgot how to breathe. There was no time to wonder why our driver wasn't reversing at the speed of light, or anything else for that matter. In fact, my entire recollection of this encounter is a blur. Did this stand-off continue for seconds or minutes? Honestly, I couldn't tell you.

When the elephant retreated into the bush, I remembered how to breathe, albeit very erratically at first. Everyone around me seemed to share my view that we'd narrowly escaped being turned into a fine powder by our disgruntled new camp mate. Our driver stuck his head out of the window and looked back to check on us with a grin on his face and a twinkle in his eye. Despite his demeanour, my hunch was that this encounter might have been a bit close, even for his liking. The people who worked out there appeared unafraid of anything. Then again, I think I'd become like that if I dangled out of helicopters and came face to face with ruthless poachers in my daily line of work. They were also deeply in tune with the bush and its abundance of creatures. Knowing when they were in danger and when they weren't was second nature to them.

A minute or so later, when we arrived at our camp, our driver jumped out and helped us off the truck. 'Close, eh!' was all he had to say about the experience as we fumbled our way down, doing our best to navigate the terrain using our now-useless legs. 'You had nothing to worry about, you know; he was just pretending,' he added.

There's such a thing as a mock charge, which is not at all like a real charge, he proceeded to explain. The first thing to know is that elephants do both, and the ability to accurately read which one you're dealing with can mean the difference between life and death. A mock charge is a grand display, nothing more than a show of power. Exactly as we'd just experienced, the animal will trumpet, flap its ears, sway, and even move towards you, and it's in this moment that your actions determine whether or not the mock becomes real. It's important to hold your ground in these instances, as running or retreating is one of the quickest ways to invite the elephant to come for you. And that's where it gets scary, even for veterans of the bush. A real charge from an elephant means business, and is easily distinguished from the mock version because the ears are flat against the body, the head is down and the animal is coming full speed your way. That is the time to run.

With this less-than-reassuring image in our heads, we picked up our backpacks and the driver started up the truck. Before he pulled away, he paused and called out the window to us. 'Don't forget, that's only the elephants, yeah! No such thing as a mock charge from a rhino – if one of them's chasing you, you should have started running minutes ago!'

And just like that, I was suddenly feeling wide awake despite the fact that it was close to 11 pm. Nevertheless, my body was ready to collapse, so I was pleased to see that our bomas were only metres ahead.

This camp was smaller, and for some reason didn't seem to have the same fencing around it as the main one, but I was too preoccupied with the elephant and rhino story to give that fact much thought. It was also lush and green, shrouded in vines and tree branches, with the glow from our tiny circular huts peeking through the foliage. Fidu and I said goodnight to the group and made our way through the palm-thatched door of our boma to find a cosy and welcoming sight. It was beautiful. The space was barely big enough for the two beds, which were made with soft, cotton sheets and draped in mosquito nets. There was a small desk, pushed against the wall, with a nightlight for each of us. The walls were mud, which meant that the bomas stayed cool even through the crippling heat of the day, and walking into them at night was the next best thing to taking a cold shower. And should you want both, the showers were a quick dash through the trees to the other side of the camp.

Despite this comfort, it was no trouble to dive out of bed at the crack of dawn with sheer excitement about what the day had in store. Looking back, I doubt that we got more than four or five hours of sleep a night for the entirety of the course. Most days would start around five in the morning, when the utes would be waiting for us outside our bomas, and then finish in the evening whenever the work was done, which was usually around ten or eleven. In hindsight, I'm sure we were running on adrenaline for most of it, because I have no recollection of feeling tired until our departure day, when 'tired' didn't even begin to scratch the surface of it.

On day one, experiencing the smells and sounds of the African bush on the morning drive to the main camp proved to be an invigorating way to wake up, and I felt ready for the day ahead. We scoffed down breakfast in the open-air dining room and made our way to the lecture theatre at 6.30 am when, according to the laminated timetable in our welcome bags, we were due to have our first session. Fidu and I quickly found ourselves two seats at the front of the room and took up residence here for the rest of the course. And, as happy as I was with our positioning, I was mindful of what my friend Nikki would have said had she been here with me: certainly something along the lines of my enthusiasm being a source of deep embarrassment for her.

In this opening lecture, we were introduced to the structure of the course and what the next twelve days would entail. Much of this first week would be spent in this very room, for hours on end, covering the theory behind wildlife capture and translocation: pharmacology, physiology, differences between species, capture techniques, darting systems and – a new topic for me altogether – the aerodynamics of helicopter flight. In essence, this part of the program was crammed with everything we'd need to know in order to safely and successfully complete the following week of field work. There'd be plenty of practical sessions in this time, too. A quick scan of the itinerary revealed that we'd be spending our afternoons doing darting practice, helicopter work, post-mortem examinations, CPR sessions and everything else in between.

Over the next few days, we sped through the essentials of wildlife capture and translocation, and covered topics I couldn't have conjured up in my wildest dreams. Of course, we started with some of the basics, like the drugs we could and couldn't use on certain species and in certain conditions, but even these topics were conveyed with a flair peculiar to veterinary medicine. For instance, we studied one drug which is so powerful that if any of it brushes against your skin, that simple contact can cause your heart to stop in under a minute. Because it's used so commonly in these settings, not only was a thorough understanding of it necessary, but so were the resuscitation techniques needed to revive a colleague, should they be exposed to it. Given that there were so many opportunities for such a thing to happen here – from spilling some in the helicopter while trying to load a dart to unknowingly touching the animal where drug residue may be left over from the dart site – exposures can, and do happen, and far more frequently than I would have thought. One of the course leaders, for example, accidentally splashed himself a few years prior while following an elephant on foot through scrubland. Luckily, he had packed some of the reversal medication and immediately injected himself in his leg. About three hours later, he was found by his teammates sitting by a tree, totally disorientated. It took almost a week for him to recover, and then he discovered that not only did he have no memory of the days after the exposure, he had no recollections from the three days before it! It certainly is a potent drug, but then again, I guess that's what you want when trying to bring down an elephant, rhino or giraffe.

This same drug, which I am choosing not to name here, is lethal in the hands of the wrong people. For one, it is favoured by poachers for illegally immobilising rhinos in order to harvest their horns. It has also been used on humans. There was a horrific incident in Moscow in the early 2000s. A group of terrorists ambushed a theatre in Russia's capital, taking 850 hostages in what would become a four-day siege. By the third day, the Russian government was desperate to resolve the situation and formulated a plan to enable the safe retrieval of both hostages and terrorists. An anaesthetic gas was filtered through the theatre's ventilation system; the intention was to temporarily incapacitate everyone inside. What resulted, however, was the near-immediate death of 204 people, and hospitalisation of over 600 others. While the exact substance used has never been divulged by the Russian government, despite pleas from medical professionals who were attempting to treat survivors at the time, it was later rumoured to be this exact drug – an elephant anaesthetic – in gaseous form.

Another drug caught my attention in the pharmacology unit, although thankfully for entirely different reasons. Colloquially known as 'Scoline', mainly because its full name is too tricky to pronounce, it works by paralysing the body's muscles. And, as alarming as this sounds, it can be extremely effective in certain scenarios in both human and veterinary medicine. In the human medical world, Scoline is frequently administered to ensure that an anaesthetised patient stays perfectly still during a delicate operation, removing the potential for involuntary twitching and reflexes. In our vet world, it makes a great anaesthetic agent in some of the more unusual species, such as crocodiles and alligators (where, as you might imagine, it's critical that they're unable to move while we're working on them).

Scoline is becoming less and less popular these days, as new and improved muscle relaxants come to market. Back in its heyday of the '50s and '60s, though, it had a particularly dangerous 'off-label' use among medical and veterinary students, who would stage 'Scoline races'. A group would gather on a start line, inject themselves in the leg with a syringe full of the drug, then run as far and as fast as they could before their muscles became paralysed. The clincher here was that Scoline paralyses all muscles – including the breathing muscles – meaning that the participants had to rely on friends to keep them breathing by performing mouth-to-mouth resuscitation until the medication wore off ten to twenty minutes later! Now that's trust, or perhaps, more accurately, stupidity. Of course, every good competition has a winner and naturally, once recovered, the one who'd made it the furthest before collapse would be crowned champion.

In physiology class, it was time to learn about the individual animals, from how they worked at a cellular level right through to their behaviour alone or in a group. This class was littered with detail that would put my entire six years at uni to shame, and that loaded us up to the eyeballs in information within a couple of days. We learned compatible drug combinations for each species, and mastered exactly why each combination worked. As I would experience the following week, giraffes, for example, have a tendency to run themselves to exhaustion – and, subsequently, death – if they aren't brought to the ground in a matter of minutes. Going against almost everything you aim to do as a veterinarian, you must give the animal such a huge overdose of the immobilisation drug that it practically comes straight down to the ground, often with its heart stopping in the process. This is one of the reasons that giraffe capture is so exhilarating and intense. To counter the way in which you've brought down the giraffe involves a sprint through the bush, a lot of fancy rope work at the feet of the galloping animal to break its fall, an immediate injection of the antidote, and, if necessary, an electric prodder to restart the heart. It remains, today, one of the most unbelievable things I've ever been involved in, and never fails to make me feel like I could do with a good dose of the electric prodder myself by the end of it.

As for some of the other species, there was a deluge of facts to learn that I could never have imagined coming across anywhere else but here. One of these was that lions have a tendency to remember their captures, meaning that you risk being outsmarted should you attempt to capture the same animal more than once. For this reason, the memory-addling drug that was used back in the zoo with the chimpanzees is also often the first choice with them. As I'd find out for myself just a couple of days later, lion capture is a sophisticated waiting game that involves laying a bait – an animal carcass – that has been laced with a cocktail of sedatives, a tracking device, and some (incredibly) loud speakers booming through the bush. But we'll get to that.

On the other hand, rhinos, I learned, don't appear to remember their captures. They do, however, have a few key traits that are worth keeping in mind if you'd like to come out the other side in one piece. It's extremely important to know exactly which species of rhino you're working with and plan accordingly. In the case of the confusingly named white rhino – which is actually grey – it is distinguished from the black rhino by its thick and wide upper lip. It is thought that the animal was called the 'wide rhino' by the Dutch, and that the Dutch word *wijd* was misadapted as 'white'. Of more relevance to us was the white rhino's distinctive temperament and behaviour. You could think of it as a wild, giant African puppy dog. It's known for being everyone's best friend: sociable, affectionate, playful and – most endearingly – difficult to enrage.

The black rhino is the complete opposite. It's the scary twin sister that nobody wants to approach, much less hang out with. In short, in a capture situation, a black rhino won't stop until it's killed either you or itself, so the utmost caution and skill is required when dealing with this species.

It's good to remember some basic pharmacology when it comes to the two, notably that a white rhino will come crashing down with only a sniff of your immobilisation drug, whereas a black rhino can handle it much better (further reinforcing their reputation as a creature you don't want to cross). The reverse is true when waking them up. If you aren't careful, you may have a suddenly alert and ready-to-go black rhino on your hands with just the smallest amount of the antidote – definitely not a situation you'd want to find yourself in!

Physiology continued on this way, with astounding gems of information dotted in among some of the more painful things, like blood–gas curves and all of the other highly academic topics that I'd tried, unsuccessfully, to rid my memory of following graduation. As I found out, these dry and intellectual topics are unfortunately part of the deal when signing up to become an animal doctor. They are also an undeniably critical part of the job.

In saying that, as much theory as there was to learn (both good and bad), there are some tips and tricks of the trade that just can't be found in a textbook. These are the things that you can only learn by doing, or by being told by those who *had* been 'doing' for a number of years, even decades. My favourite of these was, undoubtedly, learning the secret and unlikely weapon behind a successful cheetah or leopard capture. In class one day, the slideshow flipped to a Calvin Klein advertisement and our lecturer proceeded to tell us that keeping a bottle of the brand's 'Obsession for Men' cologne in the car was always a good idea. Apparently, and rather unwittingly I'd imagine, Mr Klein created a scent so irresistible to these spotty cats that wildlife vets now use it by the bucket-load to spray their cages and traps with. In fact, the cats love it so much that some people have gone so far as to recommend that men refrain from wearing the cologne while around these animals if they want to avoid a very personal encounter with some unwanted admirers! From my perspective, it certainly makes for a piece of African bush that has never smelt more glamorous, and I don't think I'd be the only veterinarian to extend a sincere thanks to Mr Klein for his assistance.

By this stage of the course, I was simply doing my best to keep up. As my head hit the pillow each night, my mind would be spinning with lessons, stories, near-misses and tidbits taken from the day's lectures. I'd reflect on the little things, like the fact that zebras are especially feisty and will go out of their way to bite you. Or that elephant skin is so thick that if you don't bend your needle slightly before darting them, you'll end up with nothing more than a blocked dart and a wide-awake elephant. Then there were the bigger things. Never trust a buffalo, for example – they're smart, and on recovery will limp off into the bush, only to wait for you to pass before quietly circling around to come back and charge you in revenge. As I mentioned earlier, rhinos are fast but no good at turning, meaning that aside from the issue that you should have already started running minutes prior to finding yourself with an angry rhino in hot pursuit, a jump to the side might just be enough to save your life.

As luck would have it, I'd need to test out that last fact only a few days later.

The practical

Over the following days, we moved beyond the lecture theatre and onto some of the more hands-on components of the course. These were designed to equip us with the skills to capture and translocate any animal from a wildebeest to a giraffe in a way that would mean both of us came out the other side of it unscathed. At least, that was the plan, but in these unpredictable and high-stakes endeavours, sometimes things don't go as expected.

We eased into these practical sessions with an introduction to conducting autopsy exams, which is sadly a large component of veterinary work, regardless of the setting. In the wild these examinations are critical as, more often than not, foul play is involved. They're intensely focused on establishing an animal's cause of death, and are approached in a similar manner to that of a criminal investigation. They even come with their own toolkit – one unlikely to be used by any type of veterinarian other than those who work with wildlife.

Initially, it was the scale of the undertaking that was shocking to me. Not just the sheer size of some of the animals you might find yourself conducting autopsies on, and all the practicalities that come along with such work, but also the *number* of them. Too often, deaths can occur in the tens, twenties and even hundreds, which makes for a completely overwhelming task when you think about it. Malicious poisonings, for instance, are extremely common throughout Africa, and in many areas, cyanide is the drug of choice. Poachers are notorious for laying down cyanide to poison elephants and rhinos so they can harvest their tusks and horns. As horrific as this is, the scale of the tragedy escalates because the toxin remains in the carcass, which then poisons the countless animals who feed on the remains. One administration of cyanide has the potential to cause the mass death of predators such as lions, leopards and hyenas, or scavenger species such as vultures. And, to highlight how significant this can be, a single elephant poisoning in Namibia back in 2013 resulted in the deaths of more than 600 vultures. For this reason, instant cyanide test kits are an essential part of any field autopsy. In order to ensure both human and animal safety, it's crucial to be able to establish how urgently something needs to be removed from the scene.

The day we studied this, lunch was a sombre affair as awareness of the extent of suffering we humans are capable of inflicting washed over us. I was powerfully affected by the magnitude of loss that can occur from a single poisoning, like in the case of the vultures. This is a devastating blow for an important species, one that's already being actively targeted by poachers, who regard them as pesky 'alarm bell' birds. Because of their natural tendency to congregate and circle over an animal in the wild that appears sick, is stumbling or has perhaps even gone down, vultures 'sound the alarm' to others in the vicinity that something's happening and simultaneously pinpoint the location.

Many of us in the field turn this behaviour to our advantage by watching vultures in order to track our darted animals: those that move in a herd can be difficult to locate among all the action. For poachers, on the other hand, vultures are their worst nightmare. They draw attention to what's often the scene of a crime, such as when a rhino has been illegally immobilised in order for its horn to be brutally harvested, and it's been left for dead. Because vultures are so quick to arrive, they give anti-poaching rangers a chance to catch the criminals in the act and, if lucky, spare the animal's life.

Considering the morning we'd had, it was a relief to have something to look forward to that afternoon – I'm sure

I wasn't the only one keenly anticipating the scheduled class. After several theoretical lessons on the topic, it was finally our chance to be introduced to the range of dart guns and learn how to use them.

After lunch, we made our way from the dining room out through the wooden gates of the camp and down into a nearby section of bush where several tables had been set up for us. On closer inspection, it almost felt like I was walking into an army barracks, given the amount of weaponry and machinery around. Each of the five trestle tables sitting among the scrub was piled high with different dart guns and a mind-boggling selection of darts. The plan, we were told, was to first learn how to construct a dart (which was far less self-explanatory than I'd expected) and then how to load it correctly into the gun. From there, we'd spend the afternoon taking aim at the targets that our instructors had dotted throughout the bush about 25 metres away.

The first lesson of darting, keeping in mind the potency of the drugs used, is to ensure you've put your dart together perfectly. This includes not splashing the drug around as you're trying to get it into the syringe, and screwing together each component in precisely the right way. Should you get a step wrong, chances are you've just built a missile full of elephant anaesthetic which, rather than projecting out the front of your gun, is likely to explode out the back ... onto you. While I was no expert on the matter yet, by now I knew enough to realise that this was a scenario that was best to avoid. There was, however, a surprising amount of stuff involved in dart assembly, and handling it all correctly and getting each step right was far easier said than done. That afternoon, I hung on every word that came out of the instructor's mouth, and sometime before nightfall, I was finally starting to get the hang of it.

After a good night's sleep, and with fresh minds and full stomachs, we returned to the tables bright and early, ready to give it another go. The entire morning was set aside for this activity, and at least in my case, I had no doubt that all of that time would be needed. I marvelled at the commitment of the instructors who'd been tasked with transforming this group of novices to a point where we'd be able to hang out of a helicopter and safely shoot some of the most dangerous drugs in the world into some of its most dangerous animals.

Methodically, we progressed through the different darting systems and firearms, learning the secrets to each as we went. We revisited the drug combinations that could and couldn't be used together within the dart itself, and discussed every scenario we could conceivably face when out in the bush alone. We also revisited the physics of flight and did our best to understand all the ballistic factors involved in getting a dart from a gun and into an animal – which, as I was coming to understand, was no small feat. Chances are that you'll be taking aim from the open door of a fast-moving helicopter or from the back of a speeding truck, but your target is unlikely to be so obliging as to remain stationary. Your head is spinning from rapidly calculating things like the animal's weight – and therefore the dose of drug needed – skin thickness, response to immobilisation and general physiology, and you're also contending with the elements.

Even assuming I could load the drug into the dart with a steady hand while under those conditions, I couldn't imagine that dart making it anywhere close to an animal. Here, in this controlled setting, maybe, but achieving accuracy while managing those variables seemed to require superhuman prowess. Yet it seemed that the instructors had considered all this, and they had come up with a solution.

Her name was Jessica.

I was introduced to Jessica later that day as we gathered in a clearing about twenty minutes from camp. We'd been told that a long afternoon was ahead of us, although we were still unsure what to expect. A lot of our schedule had to be adaptable, as it was heavily dependent on things like the weather, particularly the ambient temperature. Captures can only be done at certain times of the day – usually first thing in the morning or very late at night. This is to avoid putting the animal through undue stress from the heat of the day. Another factor to consider when timing your capture is when your animal of interest is likely to be most active. It's no use trying to capture a leopard in the middle of the day when it's usually asleep and completely uninterested in your bait, even *with* the assistance of Mr Klein.

After loading up on lunch and slathering ourselves with sunscreen, we piled into the back of the trucks and took off into the bush. As we sped through the scrub, I gripped the handles along the tray of the ute. My feet would leave the floor each time the vehicle tore over tree roots and rocks, and it wasn't too much of a stretch to imagine someone flying off the back if they weren't paying attention. We were nowhere near the track, let alone a road, and at one point the bush became so dense that the visibility for the driver must have been pretty much nothing. How drivers could navigate through such a thing was nothing short of incredible, not to mention a whole lot of fun. Tree branches whipped past us, squealing their way along the body of the truck as they went, and within a minute or so,

I'd completely lost sight of the two other groups that had left camp with us.

Eventually, we skidded into a clearing and realised what the instructors had in store for us. Sitting there was a small black helicopter, and standing alongside it was a beaming pilot. He'd obviously been waiting for us to arrive and began waving his hands enthusiastically in the air when we burst out of the scrub. As we got closer, I could see a ute next to him decorated, quite elaborately, with colourful streamers; a thick plank of rubber was securely strapped to the roof. I was looking at the famous 'Jessica'.

Jessica – a distinctly female form that had been painted onto the upper surface of the rubber plank – was our target for darting practice. Not only was she hard to miss but everything about her was incongruous, although that was probably by design. From the fluorescent paint used for her outline to the features of the outline itself, there was nothing subtle about Jessica. Putting two and two together, I surmised that we'd be chasing her from the air.

All of us jumped out of the utes and gathered around the pilot, who proceeded to give us an introduction to the aircraft. It was a Robinson R44, a well-known capture helicopter. Compact and light, the R44 is easy to manoeuvre through the terrain and adept at changing direction, which is exactly what you need in such a situation. Already, we'd taken classes on helicopter flight, so I was aware that what we were about to do came with a questionable-at-best safety rating. From these lessons, the topic that lingered in my mind was the 'dead man's curve', a name that's rather difficult to ignore. It denotes a curved region on a chart that compares altitude with airspeed: certain combinations – such as low speed and very high altitude or, apart from take-off, very low altitude – are unsafe to operate in, and are depicted as shaded areas. What I took from this class was that wildlife capture work is almost exclusively performed in these shaded areas, the very ones that anyone training to become a helicopter pilot is taught to avoid. At the low altitudes required for wildlife capture, not only are you contending with low-lying trees and powerlines, but the aircraft has scarcely any energy to recover quickly enough from an emergency situation.

During that time, I fleetingly questioned my chosen vocation. However, if you wanted to work with wildlife – especially in Africa – there was next to no way around it. Helicopters are used out here the way we'd use a car or truck at home. They're good for darting animals from the sky, and helpful in finding and herding them towards a team that may be waiting on the ground to capture them. In other instances, helicopters are also great for transporting animals that are found in areas inaccessible by road. Smaller aircraft, like the one I was about to hop into, are frequently used to rescue elephant or rhino calves that have found themselves alone and in need of assistance. And, while I'm yet to experience what it's like to fly in the passenger seat with one of those animals across my lap, I'm very much looking forward to the day.

Once it was time for us to get going, I did my best to put the dead man's curve out of my mind. Our pilot had finished his safety briefing, and the ground team introduced the plan for the afternoon. As I suspected, we'd be taking our darting practice to the sky, and learning what it's like to not only shoot from up there, but to be aiming for a rapidly moving target. Jessica's driver had been tasked with charging ahead of us, up the dirt airstrip and through the bush as we took chase in the chopper. And, since a bit of healthy competition never goes astray, the person to get their dart closest to the bullseye had a bottle of spirits waiting for them on the ground.

For whatever reason, the only part of the briefing that I'd thoroughly caught was to be careful of the rotors on your way in and out of the helicopter, and under no circumstances to raise your hands or firearm anywhere near them or you'd risk losing both. Once my turn came, I folded my tall frame in a ridiculously stooped fashion, almost as if I was about to climb into my nephew's cubby house, and clambered into the aircraft. Once I was strapped in, with one very loose strap around my waist – which felt much like being in the middle seat in the back of an old car – we took to the sky. I'd been lucky enough to have been in a helicopter before, although comparing this with the previous experiences was like comparing apples and oranges. For one, there were no doors this time, and the rush of the wind and the sound of the rotors were so overpowering you could barely hear yourself think.

Within moments, we were travelling at speed yet still close enough to the ground that you could clearly make out everything below. The chopper darted through the trees, dropping up and down as we went, following the car which, just as a herd of antelope might, was leaving a thick cloud of dust behind in its wake. I edged my way to the door, dart gun in hand, and slowly slid my legs outside, checking the seatbelt once more as I went. I didn't have time to wonder if the flimsy little strap would be enough to catch me if I lost my footing; I just had to hope. The pilot informed me, through our headsets, that Jessica was heading for the clearing and he was going to drop down on top and tilt my door towards her to give me a shot at the target. I was in awe of his skill, as well as reaction times, as there really was no more than a second or two between these decisions and the manoeuvres.

A minute later – though equally it was as though an hour had gone by – I'd taken my shot at Jessica and we'd made it back to the ground. The time in the air was a blur of action and movement, wind and noise, and I wouldn't have had a clue if my dart had even left the gun, let alone come into vague proximity to the target. To be dangling from the open door of a helicopter, metres from the ground, with a dart gun in hand is an experience that remains, to this day, difficult to describe. But, for this very first experience, it's near impossible. I remember being so exhilarated by the whole thing that it really didn't concern me where my dart had ended up. By some stroke of luck, it turned out that it had not only successfully left the gun but had even found its way to Jessica. No one was more surprised than me, and when I say that it was a stroke of luck, I mean it in its sincerest form. If anything is testament to this, it would have to be the fact that a short six months later, while at a conference in the USA, I repeatedly failed to get my dart to make contact with a wooden board a mere 10 metres away. And that was sans helicopter.

Once everyone had finished taking their shots at the target, we gathered in the clearing to debrief about our experience in the air. The thing that had struck me the most about it all was just how fast things move in a capture scenario, particularly from the vantage point that we'd had. Jessica had given us an idea of how quickly and erratically an animal can move through the bush, and how challenging it can be to be in pursuit of such a thing. Of course, darting from a helicopter isn't your only option when planning to capture an animal. The choice you make can vary greatly depending on which species and how many of them you aim to catch.

While capturing an entire herd in one go was another matter for another day – more specifically, something I'd be focusing on a bit later in the year in South Africa – that wasn't something we had time to go into here. For now, we needed to redirect our focus to the captures each team would be completing over the following few days. For me, this was the giraffe. And, if today was anything to go by, it wasn't exactly going to be a walk in the park.

The captures

Catching a giraffe in the wild is every bit as difficult as it sounds: extremely.

I'd woken up at about four in the morning, charged with adrenaline, wondering how the day would unfold. If I'm being honest, by this stage, I was suffering the effects of exhaustion.

All of our studies, training and practical sessions had been leading up to these final days of the course in which each team would be responsible for the capture and translocation of their allocated species. For me, that meant today was the day I'd be catching a wild giraffe in the middle of the bush. Well, that was the plan at least.

In class, we'd learned the basics of what it would take to bring a giraffe to the ground in a safe and careful manner. We'd touched upon the topic of the deliberate overdose, and I was aware of the electric prodder situation – alarmed about it, too. We'd also studied, in depth, the chain of events a giraffe capture entails. In the space of a few minutes, we'd locate the individual animal (which is usually moving as part of a herd), dart it, get it to the ground using ropes, apply earplugs and blindfolds, get it back *off* the ground, and then coax it to walk, with the ropes, into a truck. It's also worth mentioning that after the animal has been darted with the overdose, and subsequently had the anaesthetic reversed, it then becomes a matter of keeping a fully conscious, 800-kilogram giraffe on the ground while we finish our work. Easy.

Lectures aside, it was out of the classroom that I really began to appreciate just how technical, challenging and physically demanding such a thing might be. In the days leading up to the captures, we'd split into our respective groups before bedtime for a debriefing on the things we could expect. Additionally, the giraffe team, which had to manage a high level of complexity, was required to do a series of 'mock captures' in which we'd essentially role-play the entire thing from start to finish. To do this, we needed a helicopter team who'd be responsible for finding and darting the animal, a ground team who were tasked with catching it, and, of course, a giraffe. Should any onlookers have been lurking in the nearby bushes, it would have been the most absurd bit of acting they'd ever witnessed. It certainly was for me.

On the night before the capture, we gathered at the reserve's old airstrip and decided who'd play what in the role-play. For some reason, I'd put my hand up for the giraffe, and that's the part I ended up with in this charade. Meanwhile, the others had, wisely, stayed quiet and consequently landed themselves with far more respectable positions. While they loaded themselves into the back of the truck, ropes in hand, I was simply given the instruction: 'Run'. My only task was to evade the truck, and being far from a natural-born runner, I wasted no time in charging off into the bush as fast as I could. On a signal from the helicopter team, the truck took off and gave chase. I still can't help but think what a sight this must have been. Within no time at all, the truck screeched to a halt just ahead of me as the team jumped out and continued their pursuit on foot. It was their job to use two pieces of rope to bring me down in a highly choreographed manoeuvre that resembled a rather unusual dance I was made to learn in school called the 'Maypole'.

Incredibly, this modified-Maypole move involves waiting for the giraffe to make contact with your ropes, and then weaving your way around its legs – while it's still running – to bring it to a halt. We did our best to replicate this, although I had a feeling that no amount of practice was going to adequately prepare us for the real thing. Then again, I doubt anything would have.

It was around 7 am the following day when we regrouped at the airstrip, ready for the capture. The air was crisp and cool, and it echoed with the sound of the local army of anti-poaching rangers performing their morning practice. This was a usual sight on the reserve, as well as on many of the neighbouring properties, with most of them now employing their own anti-poaching teams in an effort to combat the relentless assault on their rhino populations. Just keeping rhinos on your land has become not only a dangerous exercise but also a costly one, as adequate protection like this is not cheap.

Our task was to capture and translocate a large male giraffe that had been monitored by trackers for the past couple of weeks. Conditions on the reserve had been worsening in the drought, and it had been decided that this individual would need to be moved to a more suitable area to ensure his welfare. In the process, we'd also be taking a blood sample for routine disease surveillance as part of a wider program monitoring the overall health of the giraffe herds in this region of Zimbabwe.

We were ready for the capture – all drugs had been drawn up and loaded into the darts, the trucks were packed, and the helicopter team was waiting for the signal to launch. As they took off, the rest of us loaded ourselves onto the trays of the trucks, held on tightly to whatever we could find, and sped off into the scrub. In such dense and bumpy terrain, well away from any semblance of a road, we relied entirely on the directions being radioed through from the team above. Over the following minutes it was our job to keep close enough to the action so that we could swoop in quickly once the animal had been darted, but keep far enough away so as not to interfere with the process. In what felt like no time at all, we'd received the call that the helicopter team had successfully darted the giraffe, meaning that the clock was now ticking for us to get to it. If it was not brought to the ground quickly, it would run the risk of overexerting itself, potentially leading to disastrous consequences. Alternatively, if it were to collapse to the ground without us being there to break its fall with our ropes, the animal could suffer serious physical injury.

We clung on to whatever we could find as the truck tore through the bush in search of the darted giraffe. Seconds later, it appeared out of the scrub, galloping down a clearing at full speed and already starting to appear unsteady as the sedative took effect. The driver of our truck accelerated towards the giraffe as we began the chase, reaching up to 70 kilometres an hour while dodging rocks, bushes and other animals to get ahead of it as it thundered down the open plain. Within moments, the driver had skilfully manoeuvred us into a position mere metres ahead of the stumbling animal and gave the call for us to dive out of the vehicle and into the scrub.

Running as fast as I could, I dashed to the other side of the clearing, rope flying out behind me as my partner held on tightly to the other end. We braced ourselves for impact on either side of the rope as the giraffe continued towards us. With luck, the animal wouldn't veer off course in the last moments.

In that instant, I had two realisations. While it may seem obvious, the first was how positively enormous these animals are and how extraordinarily fast they move. Until then, I'd always considered giraffes to be graceful and majestic creatures, almost as if they only ever ran in slow motion. On the contrary, they're exceptionally fast – easily reaching speeds of 60 kilometres an hour with those impossibly long legs.

The second realisation was how little resemblance there was between our current situation and our practice sessions back at base camp. Out here, the ground was uneven and littered with obstacles like bushes and rocks that we either had to jump over in the rush of action or divert around, taking time we simply didn't have when there was a heavily sedated giraffe barrelling towards us in top gear. Additionally, not only did we have other animals to contend with now that we were out in the wild, but our giraffe was also moving in a highly unpredictable manner. Again, this was nothing like how our practice sessions had been over the past few days. Far from moving in a straight line at a constant speed – as, for instance, when I'd role-played the giraffe – this giraffe was zigzagging towards us at a phenomenal speed. It was impossible to know where to station ourselves in order to 'catch' it.

But before I could add to my mental list of ways our practice sessions had failed to prepare me for the real thing, the giraffe had made contact with our ropes. It effortlessly pulled us along with it for what felt like an eternity until we managed to break its forward momentum – coming to a screeching halt several hair-raising seconds later in the middle of the clearing. With the stationary giraffe now swaying metres above our heads, we dashed around its thrashing legs to carefully entangle the animal and bring its entire 6-metre body to the ground as safely as possible.

Out of the blue came yet another realisation. At this point, if the animal was to stumble or fall, getting out of its way would be no casual matter. You couldn't simply jump to the side, as you might do to avoid colliding with a smaller animal like a zebra or antelope. Instead, it would be more like running away from a crumbling wall – you're going to have to clear a lot of ground in a few seconds before you're out of the danger zone!

Interrupting my thoughts, suddenly the giraffe was on the ground quite miraculously (and without any of us underneath it) and the antidote was being administered into the enormous jugular vein running along the side of the animal's neck. The medication we were using was designed to completely reverse all effects of the sedative, and the giraffe was awake again within moments. Without wasting any time, four of us sprang onto the long and sprawling neck, providing just enough weight to remove any leveraging power from the animal and preventing it from getting back to its feet. Prior to this, I'd been sceptical that this was all it would take to keep such an enormous creature on the ground. Such doubts disappeared.

From my position at the top of the neck, I was able to quickly blindfold the giraffe and stuff giant plugs into its ears to remove any stimulus that could startle it. From here, I felt the animal persistently attempting to rise; my knees would briefly leave the ground each time it did. This reminded me of an anecdote I'd heard years earlier from another vet, Dr Peter Morkel, who'd been in my position on the neck of a giraffe. Somehow, he found himself alone there and, without the added weight of his missing-in-action teammates, the giraffe got to its feet and galloped off into the scrub – taking him along for the ride! His only option, he'd told me, was to close his eyes, let go of the neck and curl up into a ball – hoping that one of the enormous legs wouldn't get him on the way down. Thankfully, he lived to tell the tale, and the story will live on for what I'm sure will be generations to come (not to mention it's at the forefront of my mind every time I find myself sitting on a giraffe's neck)!

Doing my best to get this story out of my head, I returned my focus to what was happening around me. For those of us on the neck, our main priority was staying there while the rest of the team got to work. Within a couple of minutes, they'd taken all the necessary blood samples, removed the dart and rearranged the ropes so that the giraffe was ready to stand back up. On the count of three, once the team was in position and had a tight hold on the ropes, those of us on the neck dived off and made a run for it, knowing that we had only seconds to get out of the way as the giraffe thrashed its way to its feet. The instructors had assured us that at this stage, once standing, the animals were usually quite relaxed and easy to 'drive' with the ropes. And, apart from some kicking on the way up, this largely proved to be true with our giraffe. From there, we walked the animal, with its blindfold and earplugs still in place, the short distance to our truck and started on the journey to the release site.

Apart from getting a few odd looks from other drivers – no surprise when you're heading along the road with a giraffe, rhino or elephant on the back of your vehicle – the ride was uneventful. Most importantly, our passenger remained calm throughout. In saying that, he needed little encouragement to leave once the trailer doors were opened. I climbed the 6 metres to the top of the trailer, whipped off his blindfold, pulled out the earplugs and watched him lope off into the distance, looking once more like the majestic and slow-moving creature I'd always pictured.

Keeping the momentum going, that evening we gathered once more at the airstrip for what was perhaps the second most adrenaline-fuelled capture of them all: the rhino capture. As we were well aware by this stage, rhinos are one of the most commonly captured animals in Africa – usually in response to the imminent and very real threat of poaching. They are often captured to enable their transfer to hospital following a poaching attempt, or to facilitate their translocation to a more secure area. In some instances, an entire group may be moved in order to establish a new breeding herd in a protected location. However, the objective isn't always to move the animal. As was the case that night, it may be to perform a medical procedure in the field, such as the surgical removal of their horn for the animal's own protection, or to make a small notch in their ear as part of an identification program.

When translocating a rhino, there are a few more options available than with a giraffe. It's possible, of course, to move them by foot or truck, and even to fly them by helicopter or plane. Translocation by foot is certainly an impressive undertaking, especially considering the delicate cocktail of drugs required to make the animal amenable to handling while remaining conscious enough to put one foot in front of the other. In my opinion, the most spectacular of these translocations is unquestionably that by helicopter.

Black rhinos are the more likely of the two species to be translocated by air, as they mostly inhabit thick and inaccessible bushland, making it almost impossible to get to them by road. In these cases, once the animal has been darted, it's then quickly suspended by its feet to the underside of a helicopter. They are usually in the air for no more than ten minutes – just enough time to get them out of their naturally challenging terrain and onto a truck to continue the journey. Alternatively, depending on the situation, they may also be released directly from the landing place into new terrain.

Namibia-based veterinarian Dr Peter Morkel devised this feat of engineering, aerodynamics and conservation after rigorous studies on the physiological effects of suspending a rhino by its feet, not to mention help from some fellow wildlife vets who were eager to be hung from a helicopter themselves in the name of science! Using this technique, they've now successfully translocated more than 200 rhinos to poaching-protected regions, where the animals go on to form new groups of about twenty – a number considered genetically viable for the species.

My role in the rhino team's capture this evening was mostly observational. The team had been tasked with capturing a young female that had reached the age where her ear needed to be notched as part of the identification program. A straightforward procedure was planned, with no more than forty minutes between darting and recovery. With rhinos, the trickiest part of the whole undertaking was the latter. Although we were dealing with a white rhino rather than a black one, extreme caution was still necessary: this otherwise placid species won't hesitate to show aggression if threatened. And while this would be my first close encounter with a white rhino, I presumed that waking up from an unwelcome procedure wouldn't bring out the best in them.

We were accompanied by a team of armed anti-poaching rangers who'd be responsible for ensuring our safety throughout the procedure. They were equipped with AK-47 rifles that made our dart guns look like toys. These rangers were also, in effect, personal bodyguards for the rhinos, spending much of their days following them on foot through the bush. They knew exactly where to look for them. The helicopter team had been directed to the herd's location, and the rest of us waited on the ground for the call that our target had been darted. Then, once it had come through, it was time to move.

Our target happened to be accompanied by her mother. Although the mother kept a safe distance from us, we were on edge: between the threat posed by an adult rhino looking on and knowing that a potential poacher was also lurking in the bushes – plus what we were actually there to do – there was a lot on our plate. Thankfully, the procedure went exceptionally quickly. Our clinical examination, blood sampling and ear notching were all completed within the first twenty minutes. The young rhino remained stable throughout the anaesthetic, and Mum even stayed relatively happy where she was.

Next we moved to the recovery stage. It was imperative that our young patient recover quickly and find her way back to Mum. To this end, the rangers would be staying with the pair for the rest of the evening to ensure they reunited and didn't run into any trouble.

It appeared we were on track for a roaring success. But then, after we'd administered the reversal, packed up our equipment and started to head back to the car, things started to go pear-shaped. Once she'd woken up, which happened relatively quickly, she appeared to make a beeline for her mum. As described in the opening to this book, she must have made a U-turn at some point and headed back towards us. I say 'must have' because I was oblivious to her movements until it was very nearly too late. The first thing I noticed was my colleagues suddenly ditching their equipment and sprinting for the surrounding trees. Still I didn't twig to what was happening. Next, there was a soft pounding on the ground somewhere behind me and I realised, with a start, that I was the only person standing in the middle of the clearing. Now I got it! I could all but feel the ground vibrate under my feet and the little rhino's breath on the back of my neck. I broke into a run, despite knowing that it was pointless, and it was then, miraculously, that I remembered the advice I'd received about a rhino's inability to turn suddenly. I dived to the left and scrambled to my feet just in time to watch her rocket past me, missing me by a whisker. As the dust billowed behind her, I quickly climbed a tree, so by the time she'd come to a stop and turned back to find me, I was nowhere to be seen. It was the first and last magic trick I ever hope to perform with a rhino.

It took me the rest of the evening to come down from this near miss. To my disappointment, they didn't have wine back at the camp, otherwise I'd have been bottle-deep in it by the time dinner came around. How incredible that a passing comment on one of the first days of the course had been enough to save my life. What if there were other little bits and pieces I should have paid closer attention to along the way! I guess it was one way to learn and, on a more positive note, I can also now say with confidence that rhinos are, indeed, poor turners.

The elephant capture, which took place the next morning, was nothing short of a leisurely affair compared to what I'd gone through with the rhino. We'd set off, again, at around seven in the morning and arrived at our destination about half an hour later. The elephant in question had broken himself out of a national park and into a neighbouring reserve, and so required escorting back home. This was not a surprise. It seems that most call-outs to an elephant in Africa will be due to this, or because one of these troublemaking behemoths is in the process of destroying a farmer's crop. As I'd learned, elephants are considered a pest in most places here – known for breaking through fences, entering private properties and destroying everything along the way. For wildlife vets, it's important to respond to calls for help quickly in order to prevent escalation into violence between the community and the elephant. Then again, some people just don't need us at all, and I was curious to meet one such individual this very morning.

She was an impressive woman of scarcely more than 150 centimetres (5 feet) in height and aged well into her seventies. As the owner of the reserve, she was now also the one responsible for taking care of the intruder on her property, which is why she'd called us. Usually, she explained as we arrived, she never needed anyone's help keeping the neighbouring elephants at bay. Using a nifty trick she'd devised some years ago, she could get the situation under control herself. As I soon found out, her trick amounted to the weaponisation of the humble ping-pong ball. Rather than throw them at the elephants, which I'd imagine would be just about as effective as kindly asking them to leave, she cooked a fiery chilli sauce and then carefully injected it into the balls. If I had to best describe what she'd created, I guess it would be a type of elephant-specific pepper spray. She then loaded this ammunition into a paintball gun and shot the chilli-laden ping-pong balls at any elephants that looked like they were considering breaking down her fences. And, while it may seem cruel, this tactic certainly sent the elephants running, avoiding the potential for serious violence towards them and sparing the need for a visit from us in the process.

However, her tactic hadn't seemed to work on the elephant this time, and she needed our help. The good thing was that capturing and translocating an elephant is one of the more straightforward things you can do – although that's a relative statement. Like rhinos, elephants can be darted from the ground or sky, and are then followed on foot until they become anaesthetised. They are less prone to overexertion during the early stages of anaesthesia than giraffes, making it unnecessary to chase them and bring them to ground as quickly as possible. I was thankful for this point, as I struggled to see how entangling an elephant in rope could bring it to a halt. They also respond to drugs more consistently than rhinos, making one of the main considerations when darting an elephant neither the drugs nor the animals' response to them, but the fact of getting the dart *into* them. Elephants have incredibly thick skin, meaning that you need a long needle to pierce through it. As we'd learned in our darting classes, it's also important to remember to bend the needle slightly so as to avoid it 'coring', which is when a plug of tissue enters the hollow needle upon impact and blocks the exit of the drug.

Once the animal has been anaesthetised and is on the ground, the first step is to ensure that the elephant is lying on its side. I had a flashback to my time in the zoo and remembered this point well from when there were about thirty of us trying to rock an elephant over after it had gone down on its chest. The reason for this is that elephants are the only mammals in the world to lack a vital piece of chest anatomy known as the pleural space, meaning that they rely solely on the physical movement of their chest to breathe. Should they come to ground on their front, their breathing will be severely affected, something that requires immediate intervention. The next thing to check is that the trunk isn't squashed against a tree or blocked in any way. An elephant uses its trunk to breathe, and sadly there have been cases of elephant deaths in the past simply due to the trunk being kinked or misplaced during anaesthesia. To avoid this, the trunk is straightened and a small twig from a nearby tree (or something more sophisticated, if you're not working in the middle of nowhere) is used to prop open the nostrils. A monitor is then placed on the trunk to assess the animal's breathing, and water is poured over the ears – where some enormous blood vessels are located – for assistance with heat regulation. Finally, once all of this is complete, the last safety precaution is to locate and remove the dart. The main thing to remember here is to check that it has fully deployed into the animal in order to avoid it exploding out the back onto you.

In what was a refreshing change from the unexpected twists and turns of our previous two captures, everything went to plan. The elephant was darted and came to the ground on its side, and the trunk was in the clear. Nobody was underneath it, and I hadn't seen my life flash before my eyes at any stage of the process. Based on past experiences, I couldn't help but think what a success this was.

From here, the incredible translocation process began. Just about the only way to move an adult elephant is on the back of a truck or in a plane no smaller than (suitably) a jumbo jet. The challenge is getting them into such a thing. Much like the rhino, the solution is to suspend them from their feet, but this time it's done using a piece of heavy-duty machinery rather than a helicopter. Large padded straps are applied to all four legs, and the machine hoists the animal into the sky before swinging it across onto the trailer – or at least it did in this case. I have to admit, seeing an elephant lifted in this way is one of the most extraordinary sights I've ever witnessed. In just a few minutes, all 7 tonnes are effortlessly transported from the ground, into the air, and onto the back of a truck, ready to go. The trailer is padded with tyres to prevent compression injuries from the weight of the animal's own body. The elephant is able to travel several hours under these circumstances, although fortunately for our individual, he only needed moving twenty minutes down the road – back to the national park he'd broken out of to get here.

The drive went without a hitch. This time around, I was prepared for the odd looks from other drivers. Since the elephant was anaesthetised, we travelled on the trailer with him, keeping his ears wet and making sure that we were on hand in case he decided to wake up and attempt to leave prematurely. His sheer size was breathtaking; just clambering over one of his legs to get to his ears was an acrobatic feat.

On arrival, the machinery once more assisted with getting him safely off the truck, and we reversed the anaesthetic on the spot. Over a few minutes, he got slowly onto his feet – no doubt confused about why he was back to where he began the great escape – and meandered off into the bush.

Then we also meandered – back to camp. For a change, we were in no rush. Our next capture wouldn't be until the evening, so we had a rare opportunity to do as we pleased. It was the first time in two weeks we'd had a moment to ourselves, and I used it to try to jot down some of what had happened in this time. I was writing in the same diary I'd had since leaving Australia. It lasted me – almost perfectly – until a week or so before arriving home again at the end of the year. It's also sitting next to me now, helping me try to recreate my experiences for this book.

At around three o'clock that afternoon, we assembled at the trucks ready for the last capture of the course. The past couple of weeks had been a blur. There was so much we'd learned, seen and done, and I was incredibly grateful that I'd chosen to attend. In hindsight, I couldn't have been more correct – all that time ago in Victoria Falls – in stating that I really had no idea of what, exactly, I'd signed up for.

Our lion capture would be taking place approximately 20 kilometres from camp, in a remote section of bush close to where the signal from our radio device identified the cat's whereabouts. The animal was wearing a tracking collar that had been fitted several months before as part of an ongoing disease surveillance program here in southern Zimbabwe. This evening, our task was to recapture her, take blood samples for the program and remove the collar. The blood would be used to assess for the presence of a range of diseases, including the formidable distemper virus that I'd encountered a few weeks earlier.

When attempting to capture a wild 'big cat' – whether it be a cheetah, lion or leopard – you must first consider the individual animal you plan on targeting, which determines how best to go about it. For example, it may be reasonable to dart a single, habituated lion on foot, but this may be impossible for an animal living in a more remote location. For a member of a pride, or a female with young, it may be best to avoid darting altogether, and instead use a bait or trap. For an animal like a cheetah, it may only be possible to reach them from a helicopter, the downside being that any adrenaline built up during the chase will almost certainly work against the administered medication. On the other hand, for an animal such as a wild dog, it's important to use a completely reversible anaesthesia due to the complex social hierarchy in this species. If a wild dog were to be returned to the pack while still affected by the anaesthesia, the animal is likely to lose its social standing, possibly resulting in it being killed by its own pack members.

It was about four in the afternoon when we arrived at the site and got to work assembling our capture equipment. Our lion of interest was a mother with cubs, and we'd decided that the bait method of capture would be most appropriate for her. The preparation for this was totally different from any of the other captures we'd performed in the course. There were no helicopters, no 'ground team', and – initially – not even a dart gun. Instead, what we did have was a cow carcass. It had been loaded up with a sedative and strung from a tree, making it an exceptionally unusual sight here in the middle of the bush. The medication we were using, as for the chimpanzee, was ideal for two types of patient – children and wild animals, both of whom you'd prefer not to remember the event, and possibly outsmart you on your next attempt. I couldn't help but laugh a few years later when I came across a paper about the drug in a human medical journal. It was titled 'Anaesthesia for the Uncooperative Child' and covered the basics of medicated lollipops for children; a reminder of how similar our two fields are. In fact, the only difference I could see in this instance was that our lollipop was a cow carcass, and our patient was a fully grown adult lioness!

Once our carcass had been securely hung from the tree, we used branches to block access to it from all but one side. This would position the lioness perfectly in front of us when it came time for darting. We moved quickly and quietly, always keeping in mind that we were in the presence of wild animals. Just like on all our other captures, armed rangers accompanied us should something go wrong or, in the unique case of a rhino capture, we encountered a poacher intent on retrieving the horn come what may. Upon finishing the setup, the next step was to clamber back into our trucks and arrange the vehicles in a semicircle around the bait, 20 metres or so into the bush, so as not to deter the lions from approaching. And then we waited. And waited, and waited. And waited some more. The silence was broken, dramatically, by loud, squealing, distress calls from a pig that had been prerecorded to be played over our loudspeaker system. I'd never heard about this until the very moment that the first call was sounded, at which point I nearly fell out of the truck with alarm. As I found out, however, it was necessary to lure the pride to our waiting bait. Eventually, it did the trick.

A lot of wildlife work is like this – planning, monitoring and then waiting, especially when working with elusive and intelligent predator species. It was around 11 pm when our lioness finally appeared out of the bush, accompanied by an adult male and three young cubs. The pig calls were still ringing in my ears after listening to them on repeat for the past five hours, and I was starting to think that I'd never be able to erase the sound from my memory. Despite it being pitch black, we could see their silhouettes thanks to a soft red light that was shining towards the bait from our trucks. The family wasted no time in feasting on the carcass, and about half an hour later, all of them were in a slumber on the ground. The lioness was darted with a low dose of capture drug, and then removed with caution from the snoozing group. We stationed the guards around us should the male wake up from his sleep, and quickly got to work taking blood samples and removing the lioness' tracking collar.

Throughout the procedure, I kept one eye on the lions in the distance – all that stood between them and us was a light sniff of sedative. Neither was I comforted by the rangers' presence, because if it came to the crunch, the best they could do would be to fire a round into the air, hoping it would be enough to deter the animals from having us as their second course. Happily, our work was done and dusted within about ten minutes, and our lioness was then carefully carried back to her pride. We silently removed the carcass from the tree – trying to let sleeping dogs, or cats, lie – and returned to our cars. From there, it was another half an hour or so wait until the pride came around, and at last it was time to go home.

It must have been close to one in the morning when we arrived back at camp, and I have no memory of even falling into bed. I do, however, remember being woken by the horn of our truck sounding at six. This meant we had to prepare for our exams on a mere five hours' sleep. By then, we knew better than to expect a sleep-in. Like every morning before, we scurried through the boma collecting what we'd need for the day, and then jumped on the back of the truck for the ride through the bush to the main camp.

Even in a sleep-deprived state, it was always one of my favourite parts of the day, when the air was still cold, and the sunlight was just starting to stream through the branches of the baobab trees. At camp, we scoffed down breakfast, then stationed ourselves in the lecture theatre, where we remained until the early hours of the following morning doing our exam. It was a marathon effort, befitting a marathon course, and all of us were rewarded a short twenty-four hours later: we'd passed.

The final night was a celebration, to say the least. We'd gone from being a group of strangers to colleagues and friends in the short space of two weeks, and I doubt it was an experience any of us would soon forget. And, while it was goodbye for now, our paths would cross again numerous times down the track in what, as I would find out, is a very small world.

LEARNING TO CATCH ANIMALS IN THE WILD

I woke to a momentous day. It was the day the stones I'd 'collected' in Victoria Falls would be expatriating from their home country of Zimbabwe for the very first time. I'd be lying if I said a large part of me didn't hope to be stopped at customs and told they'd have to be left behind. Alas, no luck there. My water bottle was deemed to be a flight risk, but there was no problem with eighteen fresh-out-of-the-Zambezi rocks coming along for the ride.

In hindsight, I don't know why I didn't simply turf them out of my backpack and continue on my way, my load much lighter. According to my flawed reasoning, however, the time to honourably relieve myself of this burden had passed. Of course, this was far from the case. While it felt like over a decade had gone by since the rocks had joined me on this journey, in reality, it was only a handful of weeks. It was ridiculous that I was stuck with all that extra weight. But I'd given someone my word. Rightly or wrongly, I was hostage to the crippling guilt I'd experience if I reneged on it.

So, back into the bag they went.

CENTRAL AND SOUTHERN AFRICA

8
Wild gorillas and chimpanzees

A FEW SHORT hours after leaving Zimbabwe, the rocks and I were touching down in our next destination of Nairobi, Kenya. I was taking a brief foray away from the world of wildlife capture to venture into the jungle in search of wild gorillas and chimpanzees. I'd long had a love of these animals, inspired by the likes of primatologists Jane Goodall and Dian Fossey as a child. To find them, I'd have to go west and travel into the heart of the African continent where these elusive and increasingly rare primates reside – deep in the jungles of Uganda, Rwanda and the Congo.

My plan was to join a group travelling overland from Kenya, into the mountainous and less traversed countries of Uganda and Rwanda. It was a circular loop that would see me returning to my starting point here in Nairobi in about two weeks. The group was small and we'd be escorted by an experienced local guide; we already had the permits needed to enter the gorillas' highly protected homeland. I was buzzing at the prospect of seeing these majestic animals in their natural habitat for the first time. What a privilege.

As for the chimpanzees, the only personal interaction I'd had with them was close to a year before with thirty-year-old Lola at the zoo. That experience, especially the moment leading up to it when she was less than impressed with our dart, gave me reservations about what it would be like to find myself in the middle of the jungle with a group of them. One particular comment from that day at the zoo lingered in my mind. The veterinarian told me that a chimpanzee could easily rip your arm from your body, and, unlike a number of animals capable of doing the same, the chimpanzee would likely enjoy it. Well then, I guess time would tell if I'd be returning with all my appendages.

Nairobi is a frighteningly manic mega-city that overwhelms each of the senses from the moment you step foot in it. Between the constant noise of traffic and car horns, the smell of smoke and the near impossibility of walking without bumping into other people I found myself feeling claustrophobic. Admittedly, I'd just spent an extended period in the absolute epicentre of nowhere. Then again, it was sort of comforting to be in Nairobi because I'd made intermittent trips here during my time living on the Kenyan coast. To my disappointment, despite having taken lessons in Swahili for the best part of a year, apart from being able to say *jambo* (hello) and *chapati* (a delicious local bread), nothing seemed to have stuck.

In the two days between my arrival in Kenya and the scheduled departure for Uganda, I did nothing but sleep. In a matter of weeks in Zimbabwe, I'd accumulated what felt like several years of sleep deprivation, and the need to recuperate took precedence over all else. On the morning of departure, I was starting to feel like a human being again, although my haggard outer appearance still made for an alarming sight. At the meeting point, I got acquainted with the dozen people I'd be venturing with out west.

In contrast to me, my fellow travellers were almost all fresh faced, crisp shirted and bright eyed – having recently arrived from their respective countries of residence. It was heartening to realise that we were all every bit as excited as each other for the journey that lay ahead.

Our journey to Uganda would take several days, and on the way we'd be detouring through one of Kenya's most magnificent regions – the Maasai Mara National Reserve.

When it was time to head off, we piled into a minivan and slowly but surely left behind first the city, then the roads, and soon almost all evidence of modern civilisation. The next several hours were spent driving along what must have been a dried-up riverbed. On multiple occasions, the van almost tipped over – something that might have seriously worried me if, mere days beforehand, I hadn't been leaning out of a helicopter, secured by nothing but a flimsy strap around my waist.

The land out here was drought-ridden, but the Maasai villages we passed on our way broke up the rolling brown landscape with colourful reds and blues, reminding me of my visit years before. The Maasai are semi-nomadic people of southern Kenya and northern Tanzania, known for their distinctive red and blue dress, friendly nature and traditional dance. They often live in close proximity to many of East Africa's most visited national parks, making these vibrant villages one of the most recognisable sights on the continent. Despite having lived this way for centuries, they've faced recent pressure from local government to relinquish their nomadic lifestyle as authorities attempt to reclaim the land for the expansion of national parks or sale to private investors. This has created turmoil and unrest in what was previously a peaceful corner of the world and, as the Maasai have resisted, the dispute has escalated into the violent and forcible eviction of many of them. There has, understandably, been international outrage in response, largely stemming from the fact that the Maasai's ancestral rights to the land had been previously, and formally, recognised. Sadly, this seems to have meant little, and as the dispute rages on, both the Maasai people and their centuries-old culture face a desperately uncertain future.

Much of this situation resonated with me as an Australian. In the case of the Maasai, their ability to live in drought-prone areas has seen many people advocate for their lifestyle, suggesting that they may be able to pass on valuable, traditional survival skills, such as the ability to produce food and shelter in the harshest of conditions. These skills have become more pertinent than ever in our era of increasingly drawn-out periods of drought and natural disaster. In Australia, these issues have also come to prominence, along with a growing recognition of our Indigenous people and their traditional methods of land management, which might hold the key to our future survival on a progressively drier and less habitable continent.

I'd never been to the Maasai Mara before, and was concerned that it might resemble many of the other major tourist parks these days: bitumen roads that dictate where you can and cannot drive, hordes of cars clustered at each animal sighting, and souvenir shops or galleries lining the entrance ways. I was pleased to find that this was far from the case. At this time of year, in early March, the Maasai Mara was spectacularly beautiful – flooded with wildlife, and as remote and tranquil as some of Africa's least-known reserves. We spent two enchanting days driving around this vast region, marvelling at young lion cubs playing in the long grass, observing cheetahs stalking across the plains, and seeing herds of wildebeest moving in unison as if they were a single being, like a flock of birds dancing across the sky. The animals were completely unfazed by our presence, allowing us to sit there in silence while they went about their day.

It was a near-perfect two days, marred only by one mishap that, regrettably, happened to be of my own making. On the morning of our second and final day in the park, I'd confidently stated that our van could easily make it across a steep and narrow riverbed. In hindsight, I must have been quite adamant about this, as the driver appeared to follow my advice despite his better judgement. It turned out that I was spectacularly wrong, and most of the morning was spent in the ditch, alternating between calling for help and trying to heave our vehicle out of it.

Putting this mishap behind us, we said goodbye to the Mara, its people and animals, and continued west, stopping at the bustling border town of Nakuru for supplies before crossing into Uganda. Nakuru held fond memories for one of the women in our group, now well into her seventies. Back in the 1960s, she and her husband, a prominent Dutch doctor, had set up a small hospital in this dry and remote corner of Kenya. At that time, it would have been considered an even more outlandish thing to do than it would today, and her stories from this period in her life were remarkable. They'd spent close to two decades in Nakuru, running the hospital and raising their family, and this woman had only returned home to the Netherlands after her husband passed away, to be closer to her family. It was her first time back in more than forty years, and it was incredibly special to share the experience with her.

Her story brought to mind that of another pioneering woman, Dr Catherine Hamlin, who'd grown up in Sydney in the 1940s, down the road from my grandmother. In 1958, she and her husband moved to Addis Ababa, Ethiopia, where they set up a hospital for women suffering from obstetric fistulas, a debilitating injury often sustained in childbirth. Along with Dr Hamlin's legacy, the hospital is going strong to this day, just like this one in Nakuru.

The landscape changed again as we approached Uganda, with the dusty plains of western Kenya morphing into a beautifully dense, green jungle – just how I'd imagined it to look. The seemingly endless flats rolled into hills, and the Maasai villages were replaced by small round huts with smoke rising from their chimneys. Each hut had a short, winding pathway leading to the front door, a path that was swept meticulously each morning. The care and pride that people take in their homes out here was as evident as their warmth. Wherever we went, the faces of the people we passed beamed, and children greeted us with waves.

The crossing into Uganda was a bit peculiar and reminded me of the time, years before, when I crossed from Kenya into Tanzania. On a portion of the Kenya–Tanzania border, the only rule is that you can't cross by *foot*. This presented a problem for me, having turned up with little more than fifty Kenyan shillings in my pocket and a rucksack on my back. Luckily for me, I found a couple of people with motorbikes who were willing to drive me across the 500 metres of 'no man's land'. I flung my rucksack onto one bike, myself onto the other, and made my way across.

There was no such problem with the *physical* crossing here in Uganda; the challenge was a bureaucratic one.

Sitting in the small and humid office that demarcated Kenya from Uganda was a man who looked as if he'd been stationed at this post for close to eighty years. He had the air of someone who you didn't want to mess with. I waited in line and watched as, one by one, hopeful visitors to the country were denied entry on the basis of their bank notes. Through luck, I'd read somewhere that only new US dollar bills (issued after the year 2000) would be accepted as currency for the visa. Even then, it seemed to be a roll of the dice as to whether you'd be allowed in. When it came to my turn, after offering several different banknotes and more grovelling than I'd prefer to admit to, I finally came away with my visa.

Clutching it tightly for fear that a change of heart could see it withdrawn at any moment, I retreated to the minivan. Soon we were off on our three-hour journey to Jinja, a small town on the banks of the Nile River. There we set up camp for the night.

Although brief, our stopover in Jinja was one to remember. The Nile is a vast body of water, stretching from its mouth in Egypt down to its source in Lake Victoria, a distance of 6650 kilometres, making it the longest river in the world. It was a welcome sight after the drought-ridden corners of western Kenya from which we'd just come, and I fell asleep to the sound of monkeys howling in the trees and millions of litres of water thundering over the rocks and boulders that lined the riverbank.

We set off at dawn for our lengthy cross-country drive to the chimpanzee forest in far western Uganda, right on the border of the Congo. A campsite in the small town of Masindi would be our base for the trek into the jungle in search of the chimpanzees. The drive involved climbing and weaving through the mountainous landscape, passing tiny jungle villages nestled into the foothills. On arrival at the campsite, I could already hear chimp calls echoing through the trees.

In previous times, such a long journey to see chimpanzees wouldn't have been necessary, but ever-increasing threats to their existence have seen their natural range shrink, and have even driven their extinction in four separate countries where they once lived. From having a population well into the millions, there are now fewer than 300,000 chimpanzees remaining in the wild, and this number continues to fall. According to some estimates, at the current rate of decline, chimpanzees will have become completely extinct from the wild in just fifty years.

Of course, some of the pressures on chimpanzee populations aren't unique to this species. Habitat loss, poaching for bush meat, and being caught up in the illegal but booming exotic pet trade – to name a few factors –

make a considerable contribution to the destruction of all wildlife. There are, however, some pressures facing chimpanzees that are more specific to them. This includes the spread of infectious diseases, the most notable being polio, malaria and Ebola. Far from being exclusively human diseases, it's these ailments that have, at times, been responsible for wiping out entire, individual populations of chimpanzees. Worryingly, the frequency of such outbreaks seems to only be increasing with the closer proximity in which humans and chimpanzees now live. The recent influx of tourists and researchers has also spread illness.

Since it was close to nightfall when we arrived, we quickly unpacked and assembled our tents guided by the light from our head torches. Facilities were severely limited – the campsite lacked power and a water supply, and even the guards who manned its perimeter were equipped with hand-made, barbed bow and arrows rather than the usual AK-47s. It was as if we'd stepped back in time into a truly wild and untouched part of the world. My thoughts turned back to Jane Goodall, whose pioneering work with these animals began a few hundred kilometres from this spot, almost six decades earlier. It was difficult to imagine how many challenges she faced. In the 1960s, people struggled with the idea of a young woman studying any animal, let alone one as poorly understood as a chimpanzee. It was through her work, however, that she inspired generations of conservationists, and helped to ignite a love among many people for the natural world, along with the species that inhabit it.

At around six the next morning, while still under the cover of darkness, we bundled into the van and set off. It was a short drive to where we met the trackers who would be taking us to find the chimpanzees. Their knowledge of the jungle and ability to read it were imperative to the task. In silence, we ventured into the thick terrain, cutting a path through the vines with machetes as we went. It was eerily quiet at this time of the morning, the only sounds were coming from the leaves crunching under our feet, and the occasional bird call from above.

We followed the clues left behind by the chimpanzees, hoping that they'd direct us to their whereabouts. Knuckle prints in the soil, fresh seed droppings and recent nesting sites helped to paint a picture of the troop's most recent movements. Our trackers also used sound, mimicking the drumming noises that the chimps make by banging their feet on hollowed-out tree trunks to signal to their group that they were on the move. Sure enough, a call rang out in reply from the treetops to our left. Scrambling through the dense scrub, we emerged in a clearing minutes later to be met with the sight of our first troop.

There were about twenty of them, lounging in the trees and feasting on fruits, flinging the skins unceremoniously to the ground once finished. At the base of the trees, a mother was playing with her infant and some young males were having a scuffle. Their likeness to us immediately struck me, far more so than what you can appreciate in a zoo. The way they observed us, with such depth and intrigue – it was as if we were looking in a mirror. Their intellect was evident, as were the contrasting sides of their nature. Yet the image in the mirror wasn't a particularly flattering one, and that's aside from physical appearance. Their tenderness with family members was offset by the sheer ferocity and malice that was expressed to others outside that circle. Across from the mother and infant, and down from a pair of females gently grooming each other, was a group of three or four large males screaming at the top of their lungs. They were brandishing sticks and logs, using them to batter and beat an older and weaker member of the troop. Their reputation as one of the most violent species on the planet, second only to us, became painfully clear, and the words of warning from the zoo vet flitted, once more, across my mind. Thankfully, the chimps appeared to show little interest in what we happened to be doing there.

Tearing my eyes away from this escalating scene, I noticed that several trees had been completely stripped of their bark. It only seemed to be a certain type of tree, an *Alstonia*. Being a veterinarian, and using western medicines to treat chimps when they're unwell, I was surprised to learn that chimpanzees have been running their own hospitals in the bush for thousands of years, and the *Alstonia* tree is a cornerstone of this treatment. Even more surprisingly, the *Alstonia* tree has natural anti-malarial properties, which have been discovered by both the chimpanzees and many of the people living out here. Locals, when sick with malaria, will search out this tree and crush the bark to make a tea. Chimps simply rip the bark off and chew it. This means that both groups have learned to use the same tree to cure the same ailment, bringing to my mind the One Health concept again. It exemplified just how much we stand to learn by studying human and animal health in parallel, rather than categorising them as completely unrelated disciplines.

This kind of self-medication in wild animals is called 'zoopharmacognosy'. Interestingly, the array of animals known to make use of medicinal materials is very broad. For example, orangutans self-treat arthritis by making a topical paste from a plant called *Commelina*, which has been found to have anti-inflammatory properties, and pregnant lemurs supplement their diet with *Fihamy*, another type of plant, to increase milk production. It doesn't even have to be a natural substance: sparrows have started to incorporate cigarette butts into their nests, after somehow learning that the nicotine residue impedes parasitic mites.

It was encouraging to learn this, given the fact that the medication of animals in the wild remains a contentious topic. Historically, conservationists have been happy to protect a species' habitat or to fight poaching, but they've stopped short of interfering with the animals directly. In 1966, for instance, Jane Goodall stopped a polio epidemic in a group of Tanzanian chimpanzees by hiding an oral vaccine in bananas, unleashing a backlash from conservationists that lasted for years. This attitude is now starting to wane as the threat of disease to these increasingly fragile populations becomes harder to deny.

This was a topic that would resurface again on arrival in Kabale, a small village on the shores of Lake Bunyonyi, on Uganda's south-western border with Rwanda. It was here that we'd be spending the remainder of our time in the heartland of gorilla conservation work, observing some of the most elusive and intelligent species on the planet. Just like the chimpanzees, gorillas face an abundance of threats to their existence, the vast majority of which are human-driven. They also face a number of infectious diseases, two of the most threatening to their population being the common flu and the Ebola virus. Given the most recent 2013 outbreak of Ebola, which brought home the devastation the disease is capable of causing, it may seem strange to compare these two illnesses. In gorillas, however, the flu can be almost as deadly as Ebola.

The flu poses a couple of dangers. Not only is it a common disease, spread easily and rapidly from both locals and visitors to the area, but once contracted by a gorilla, it's also often fatal. Gorillas are both highly susceptible and sensitive to the disease, which is why all visitors to the area have their health checked, and gorilla conservation efforts here are strongly focused on also maintaining the health of the *human* population. As for Ebola, while significantly less common than the flu, it's also highly fatal to these primates – even more so than it is to us. The average mortality rate in humans is 50 per cent; in gorillas, it's 95 per cent. It's estimated that over the past thirty years, including in the most recent outbreak, Ebola wiped out more than one third of the world's total wild gorilla population.

And this is where the debate about vaccination, or indeed any form of medical interference, comes up again. Prior to the 2013 Ebola outbreak, given that it was primarily a disease of poorer countries in the tropics, there was limited commercial will or value in developing a vaccine against it.

This changed in 2014, when the virus spread beyond Africa and into the western world. In late 2019, the first Ebola vaccine was released and made commercially available in a number of countries. It has proven to be effective against the disease in humans and great apes alike, although the argument against using it in wild animals remains, despite its potential to save them from the brink of extinction.

Research has shown that the vast majority of Ebola outbreaks, with the notable exception of the most recent one, stemmed from the human consumption of an infected animal carcass. This discovery came from the realisation that almost every human outbreak closely followed one in animals, particularly wild gorillas. Considering that gorillas are still readily poached for their meat, which is regarded as a delicacy in many central African countries, protecting the animals from this disease could also, therefore, protect humans. It has created an interesting dilemma that has seen the consensus move in favour of vaccinating mountain gorillas to try to curb further outbreaks, in both animals and humans, before they occur.

Our base at Lake Bunyonyi was one of the most beautiful places I'd ever seen. To get here, we'd traversed the dark, red dirt roads lining the mountain tops before starting the steep and bumpy descent through the jungle to reach our campsite by the lake. The lake itself was an impressive sight. Winding through the valleys, its shimmering blue surface gave no hint of its staggering depth: 7 kilometres. The place was pristine and untouched. To celebrate our arrival, I splashed out on a six-dollar-a-night upgrade from a tent into a luxurious lakeside hut – a decision I never came to regret.

We'd be spending time with one of only two groups of mountain gorillas left in the world. One of these lives in the Bwindi Impenetrable National Park here in Uganda, and the other in the Virunga National Park, located in the eastern corner of the Democratic Republic of the Congo and bordering Rwanda and Uganda.

This part of the world is fraught with unrest and marred by decades of civil war. The Congo is still recovering from the conflict known as Africa's First World War, triggered by the 1994 genocide in neighbouring Rwanda, which led to the loss of some five million lives between 1994 and 2003. Although peace was declared in 2003, the region has remained unstable, and many eastern parts of the country, including the Virunga National Park, are still plagued by violence from various rebel groups that continue to fight government militia for control of certain areas. Over the past decade, these rebel forces have entered the forests in which the gorillas live, seizing monitoring posts and forcing out conservationists – rarely hesitating to kill any who may resist. The rebels have now become one of the biggest threats to gorilla conservation efforts. They engage in the illegal, but profitable, trafficking of baby gorillas and frequently kill the animals for bush meat. Sometimes, they kill out of pure malice.

As for the rangers of the forest, whose role is to protect the animals from such conflict, their job has been named as one of the most dangerous in the world. They risk their lives on a daily basis, and in the past ten years alone, almost 200 of them have been murdered in the line of duty. Stationed within the park itself, the rangers are tasked with monitoring the gorilla groups, tracking their movements and defending them against poaching attempts. They also habituate certain groups to human contact as a way of preparing the animals for encountering tourists: ecotourism is a critical source of funding for the gorillas' conservation.

As I'd learn during my time here, to habituate a wild gorilla to human contact can take years, and when one of these individuals is killed, it's perhaps even more devastating than if it were a truly wild one, given that these animals are, by nature, extremely trusting of people. They will allow a human within touching distance, and therefore stand no chance against poaching attempts unless shielded by rangers. If a dominant silverback gorilla is killed, this has a catastrophic effect on the rest of the group –

fragmenting the family unit and creating a trauma whose effects are seen for years after. For the rangers, the pain of such an episode is evident. Furthermore, the retrieval of the body is so dangerous that United Nations forces are often enlisted to escort them. As for the young gorillas left orphaned by such brutality, a veterinary team known as the Gorilla Doctors works tirelessly to find and retrieve these juveniles from the forest as soon as possible after the slaughter of their parents. They're airlifted or carried to safety, then raised and cared for before eventually being released back into the wild, the final step in what is for them a long and traumatic process.

As dire as the situation sounds, there is light at the end of the tunnel. The tireless efforts of rangers, conservation groups and veterinarians alike in the region have seen the mountain gorilla population begin to climb for the first time since the 1970s. In a significant turnaround, these animals have been reclassified from 'critically endangered' to simply 'endangered', with the world's population rising from just 700 individuals to over a thousand in recent years. Given that it was once believed that the species would be extinct by the turn of the twentieth century, this is a massive achievement.

On the morning of our gorilla trek, we left camp at around six. Our minivan rocketed along the lush mountain tops as the sun began to rise over the thick mist in the valleys below. At that altitude – about 2000 metres – the air was chilly. After skirting around Rwanda then heading north along the Uganda–Congo border, we reached our destination, Bwindi Impenetrable National Park. On arrival, we were met by a team of heavily armed rangers, who'd be escorting us into the jungle. The entire place shimmered with vibrant greens reflected from an abundance of different plants and vines, creating a scene so stunningly beautiful and tranquil that it was difficult to comprehend the horrors that had happened here over the past decades.

One by one, we were health-checked and screened in accordance with strict biosecurity regulations; anyone displaying signs of fever or illness would be unable to enter. Flashing lights and torches were also forbidden, because they trigger a violent reaction in the gorillas: evidently, they remember the days when fire was used by locals to hunt and kill them for bush meat. After a short briefing outlining the chain of command, including what to do should we run into trouble, we set off into the jungle.

I was allocated to a small group. I suspect the seven of us had been matched up on the basis of our presumed agility. Presumed being the operative word, as I couldn't help but notice that two of my compatriots were members of the Swedish army, and possessed a level of fitness that I certainly did not have. There were multiple groups of gorillas spread throughout the forest, and we were destined for the farthest one, which meant our trek was one of the more challenging of the day (not that the Swedes would have noticed). We moved off in single file, two armed guards in front and two behind at all times, which set a rather ominous tone for the journey.

Unlike the chimpanzee trek, this was more of a rigorous clamber through some of the thickest jungle I've ever seen. There was no path to follow, not even a slight gap in the foliage, and every step of the way was nothing short of a monumentally demanding effort. We scrambled through thick, untamed bush, climbed near-vertical mountain faces, and slid down muddy ravines – all the while battling 90 per cent humidity. Wading through knee-deep water, hauling each other out over fallen tree trunks and onto the other side, we continued this way for what felt like hours, the excitement and apprehension building with each minute that passed. Every sound stopped us in our tracks, a potential call from the very animal we were in search of.

In what felt simultaneously like a second and an eternity, depending on whether you measured time by anticipation or exhaustion, we reached a small clearing where we spotted the gorillas. I emerged from the bushes a mere 10 metres from a large silverback – the dominant male of the group – who sat there quietly watching us from his post. Several females lay around him, absent-mindedly picking leaves while the youngsters chased each other through the trees. It was as if I were looking at a scene from a Saturday afternoon picnic in the park, their family dynamics and likeness to us undeniable in that moment. Being there with them, in the middle of the jungle, was an incredibly emotional experience. Even the rangers, who spend every waking moment with these animals, were visibly moved.

For the next hour and a half, we observed the gorillas at close quarters, doing our best to follow them on foot wherever they went. This exposed our inadequacies for life in the bush. The gorillas ambled through the foliage and branches with ease, leaving us for dead in their wake. Being habituated animals, they were totally unfazed by our presence and went about their day as if we didn't exist.

Well, that was true for all but one. His name was Ladah – meaning 'Cheeky One' – and at just five years of age, he certainly lived up to the title. He'd frequently dart off from his mother's side and run over to our group trying to interact, exactly as a human child might. We had, of course, been told to keep a distance, but there's little that can be done when it's a gorilla who flouts the rules. Only when he caught a glimpse of his mother's disapproving glare would he throw himself into a ball and commando-roll back to her side. The rangers backed her up by meeting his playful attempts with a gentle *shoo*, but that only seemed to encourage him.

Doing my best not to react whenever he approached, I observed, awestruck, as Ladah stubbornly and deliberately defied the rangers. He'd grown up in the presence of humans and it showed. He would be living alongside them – it was necessary for his protection and survival, a sad fact of life. All I could hope, as I sat watching him, was that this double-edged sword wouldn't, one day, lead to his demise.

9
Malawi and a lion named Simba

THE SCRAMBLE OUT of the jungle was every bit as painful as the one into it. Perhaps even more so, with the knowledge that there were no gorillas waiting for us at the other end. Ladah and the group stayed in my thoughts for the entire return journey, and they've remained there in the years since. To this day, every report of a wild gorilla poaching stops me in my tracks, transporting me back to the jungle and filling me with dread at the possibility that it could have been one of them.

On the trek out, we were about halfway up a muddy ravine when the rangers came to a halt and hurriedly ushered us deeper into the bushes. Immediately, I thought of poachers, which was a reasonable assumption judging by the look on the rangers' faces. That wasn't it. The concern was, in fact, something I'd never even heard of before – a *forest elephant*. While I was well aware of the savanna elephant, the iconic African colossus known all over the world, I was unaware that they had a smaller, hairier, jungle-dwelling cousin that resided only in these mountainous regions of central Africa. This more elusive version is also extremely aggressive – one of the most aggressive animals on the continent, to be precise. Suddenly, the rangers' expressions made sense, and I found myself wondering if I'd just survived encounters with murderous wild chimpanzees and frighteningly enormous gorillas, only to be taken out at the eleventh hour by a pint-sized elephant.

As we stood there – nobody speaking – my mind conjured up an image of a hairy, trumpeting beast steamrolling through the foliage towards us. Considering we were deep in the forest, in the middle of nowhere, I didn't have much hope we'd survive such an altercation, let alone get to medical assistance if we did. I thought about the rhino in Zimbabwe and started to work out the chances of escaping two attacks in the space of two months. I hadn't got far with my calculations when we got the green light to proceed: the rangers animatedly gestured for us to follow. Their quick investigation had yielded nothing, and they were unsure whether there really had been a forest elephant nearby; perhaps it was something else. Either way, it was time to move.

We finished the rest of the trek at a pace just shy of a jog, which would have been a challenge even without the difficult terrain and stifling humidity. We skidded and stumbled our way over tree roots, clambered over boulders and splashed through the streams and waterways we'd waded across on our way in. It was a relief when we reached the truck, each of us drenched in sweat. Between the jungle and all of its residents – both welcoming and those potentially less so – it had been a morning to remember.

The drive back to Kenya's capital was an excruciatingly long one: it took two days to cover the 1500 kilometres, over which time, the landscape slowly morphed back into dusty red plains.

On arrival in Nairobi, I peeled myself out of my seat and said farewell to the group. While many of them were about to return home, my onward destination was the minuscule, land-locked country of Malawi in Africa's south-east.

The flight to Malawi, in a small propeller-driven plane, offered spectacular views of the vast savannas of southern Kenya and Tanzania, the endless tropical coastline of Mozambique and the glistening Lake Malawi – a body of water so enormous that it could easily be mistaken for an ocean. In fact, the lake itself takes up roughly one third of the country and is so remarkable that it's a UNESCO World Heritage site. The beauty of the lake, and the country of Malawi as a whole, however, is in stark contrast to the reality of life for many of its residents – at the time of my visit, the country was officially one of the poorest in the world. As we touched down in the capital city, Lilongwe, I could see dozens of shanty towns sitting along the dirt roadsides. As far as the eye could see, the streets were crammed with people. Smoke billowed from the numerous food stalls that lined the laneways, mingling with the bright red dust from the roads. It was a vibrant scene despite the evident poverty, which was confronting, even in comparison with the less-than-prosperous countries of Kenya and Uganda.

I was bound for the Lilongwe Wildlife Centre, a world-renowned wildlife rescue and rehabilitation facility on the city's outskirts. It was here that I'd be spending a month working alongside the dedicated on-site veterinary team, helping to care for their vast array of patients and resident animals. In the process of choosing the Centre, I'd done extensive research into the organisations in Africa that were accredited by a governing body known as the Pan-African Sanctuary Alliance, PASA. This body oversees the continent's wildlife sanctuaries, granting them accreditation if they meet criteria and guidelines that ensure they are providing the highest standard of care. For me, this research was a critical step in helping to guarantee that my time and effort wouldn't be spent in one of the many facilities on the continent that engaged in ethically questionable practices under the pretence of conservation. Some of the worst of these, in my opinion, are those that promote the hand-rearing of lion cubs, in the process collecting huge sums of money from paying volunteers who are eager to be involved. While the cubs are claimed to be orphans or part of a breeding program, often the reality is they've been snatched from their mothers to be raised by the volunteers, generating a big income for those involved. Then, rather than being released back into the wild – which, as hand-reared animals, is arguably impossible – they are instead released into an enclosed game reserve where wealthy tourists can pay to shoot them. The 'canned hunting' industry, as it's known, remains a common practice in many parts of Africa today, and is sadly, and often unknowingly, propped up by the large volume of unwitting volunteers seeking to participate.

In addition to being accredited, the Lilongwe Wildlife Centre is also known for its work with government agencies in developing ways to actively combat wildlife crime in the impoverished nation. As I'd discovered, wildlife crime is rife in Malawi due to its poverty, as well as its geographical position in the heart of the African continent. Furthermore, Malawi was recently named southern Africa's principal transit hub for all illegal wildlife products, making it a key link in the chain of poaching, trafficking and demand that threatens some of Africa's most iconic species with extinction. The country's relative lack of protective legislation, combined with lax law enforcement, have also contributed to its standing as a hotspot for criminal activity. The Centre has been instrumental in trying to change this, providing the government with a series of recommendations and proposals to strengthen the criminal justice system and wildlife law enforcement. The aim is to ensure that wildlife crime in the country is prevented and criminals are prosecuted.

Just a short drive from the airport, the Lilongwe Wildlife Centre is located in a densely foliaged locality in the city's east. It is simply enormous, sprawling across a vast area of thick jungle that looks so untouched, at the time it was difficult to believe it was on the outskirts of a bustling metropolis. The grounds are steep and hilly, with dirt paths weaving through the sanctuary, guiding visitors past an array of resident animals. It's open to the public every day of the year, providing a place for Malawians to come and see their local wildlife and learn about conservation issues.

At the back of the Centre, a long walk from the entrance and a near-vertical climb through a steep section of jungle, is the veterinary hospital. The staff here give medical care to the animals in the sanctuary, as well as the nearly 200 wild ones that come through its doors every year, including monkeys, hyenas, wild cats, antelopes, and the world's most trafficked animal – the pangolin. Most of the hospital's patients are either victims of the illegal pet trade, or those that have been injured in a poaching attempt or an instance of human–wildlife conflict. Following hospitalisation, many of them are successfully released back into the wild, but those unfit for release are able to live out their days in the safety of the sanctuary.

After introductions to the staff and the on-site veterinarian, I was shown to my accommodation, which was adjacent to the hospital. It consisted of a small wooden hut, not unlike the one I'd treated myself to at Lake Bunyonyi, with the bonus of a little outdoor shower out the back. I wasted no time unpacking my belongings before being taken on a tour of the sanctuary to meet some of its longer-term residents – the most captivating of whom was, undoubtedly, Simba.

Simba was an older, slim-built lion with a stiff walk, exquisite mane and truly remarkable history. The story of how he came to reside here even made international headlines at the time. From just eight months of age, he'd been kept in a small cage by a circus trainer in France, during which time he hardly saw the light of day. After seven long years of being subjected to mistreatment and isolation, a French animal welfare organisation got wind of Simba's plight and coordinated his rescue in 2012. He was placed in a temporary home in Belgium while a plan was hatched by the British-based Born Free organisation to return him to his rightful home in Africa. By early 2014, Simba was on a plane to Nairobi, and then it was on to Malawi, where he was met by a team from the Lilongwe Wildlife Centre, there to finally welcome the mistreated lion home.

That same day, Simba was taken to his new habitat, a massive natural bush enclosure within the sanctuary. A few weeks later, he was introduced to the only other lion at the Centre – a one-eyed lioness called Bella. She'd been rescued by Born Free five years prior to Simba's arrival, and came from a similar background of abuse and mistreatment. Bella had spent her life in captivity at a Romanian zoo, where she'd been starved, kept out in the snow, tormented and physically abused by visitors – cigarette butts had even been extinguished on her face and body; the scars were still visible.

On the day of their meeting, everyone gathered with bated breath, wondering how the two would get on. It was the first time in his life Simba would be meeting another lion. Bella had only come into contact with other lions on a handful of occasions herself, and wasn't known for her social skills.

When the gates dividing their two habitats were opened, the team watched in silence as the two lions came face to face. Immediately, there was growling and hissing, mainly from Bella; this was met with bewilderment and uncertainty from Simba. For the next few days, the two kept their distance until a scuffle broke out between them. Then, like magic, almost as soon as the dust settled, the pair became inseparable and remained so for the rest of their days. Theirs appears to have been a lifelong bond.

As I stood and watched these gentle giants lounging around in the sun together, it was painful to contemplate the suffering they'd experienced in their short lives. As a vet, I find that working with animals that have suffered at the hands of humans is always distressing. Paradoxically, it's often these cases that bring out the best of humanity, as the story of Simba and Bella shows. Returning these two lions home to Africa, and granting them some peace, was a monumental effort on the part of many. When made aware of their plight, members of the public donated the necessary funds for the animals' rescue and transportation. Then it was the combined work of Born Free and Kenya Airways which made the journey itself a possibility. And, finally, it was the Lilongwe Wildlife Centre here in Malawi who welcomed them in and provided a sanctuary where they could live out their days in relative freedom.

Simba and Bella's story is far from unique. Animals are removed from heart-wrenching conditions and transported all over the world on a daily basis. There's a good chance you've shared a flight with some of them – perhaps even Simba himself. I've found, since recounting this story over the years, that many people are unaware that wild animals frequently travel on commercial flights.

One of my friends has a job organising exactly that. He spends his days safely chaperoning animals from one side of the world to another for various conservation purposes, and the stories he tells are nothing short of incredible: from zebras loudly kicking their crates in the undercarriage of a plane, to lions waking up mid-flight and roaring, to

At four years old, with my best friend, Pep. We were inseparable.

During my time growing up on Lord Howe Island, a tiny paradise in the middle of the Pacific Ocean, I used to love accompanying researchers out on the water as they studied the ocean and its abundant marine life.

I credit my childhood years on the island as the reason I chose to study at vet school. Here I am with a mountain of notes – exam period was always the most dreaded time of year!

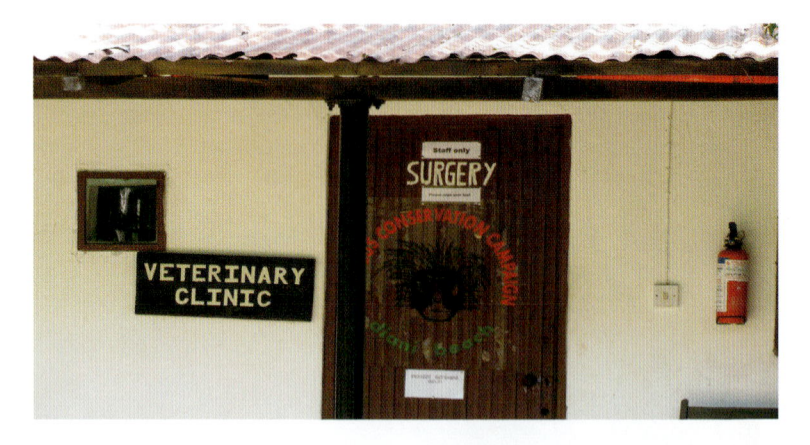

My first experience in a veterinary clinic was in rural Kenya in 2009, when I was living in the village of Ukunda.

In Africa, much of the capture work is done from the sky. For this reason, being able to dart a moving target from a helicopter is an important skill for a veterinarian working with wildlife. I'm trying to get the hang of it here in Zimbabwe!

As rhinos continue to be poached at an unprecedented rate for their horns, drastic measures are being taken to safeguard their future. This rhino has been anaesthetised and is being translocated a short distance by helicopter to a safer region.
(Photo: Dr Peter Morkel)

Safely moving a wild elephant from one place to another is no small feat. This bull had broken out of a national park and was wreaking havoc in the local community. Here we are loading him onto a truck for transport back to the park – all while anaesthetised, of course!

During a giraffe translocation, once the blindfold and earplugs have been placed, the animal is free to get to its feet. Then, with the assistance of some ropes, it can be walked into the back of the waiting truck.

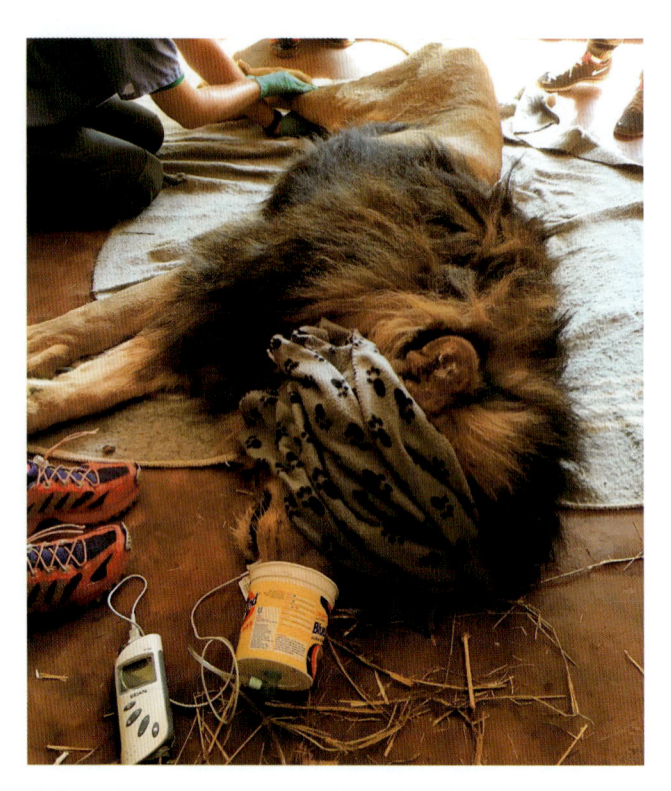

Simba – pictured undergoing a health check while under anaesthesia – remains one of my fondest encounters in the animal kingdom. He was rescued from an animal trainer in France and returned to Africa in 2014. Note the butter container turned oxygen mask: sometimes, you just have to work with what you've got!

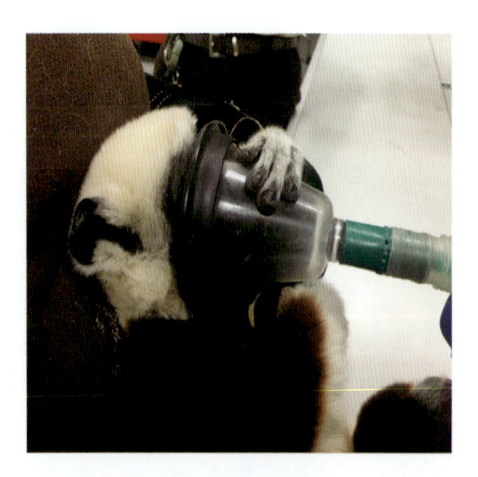

It's always a bonus when the patient decides to help anaesthetise themselves. This sifaka lemur was about to have a fracture repair on his leg after landing awkwardly on it the day before.

… And the surgery is complete! The patient is looking a bit sorry for himself but is being kept comfortable thanks to some pain medication that was hidden inside a handful of grapes.

Lion capture is an elaborate waiting game that involves laying a bait – an animal carcass – that's been laced with a cocktail of sedatives, a tracking device and some loudspeakers booming through the bush. And then, usually, some more waiting!

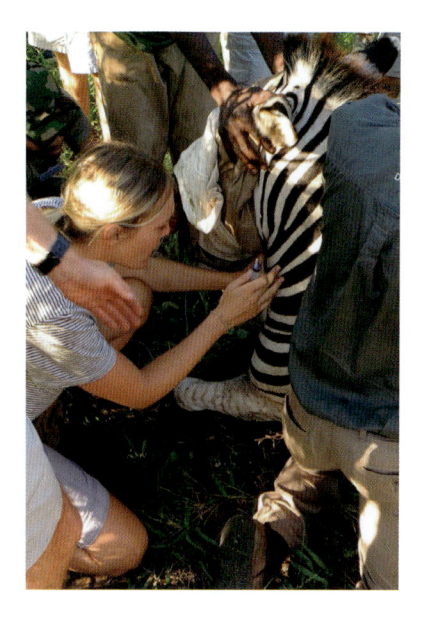

As part of a routine disease surveillance program, we were taking blood samples from the herd to which this zebra belonged.

An endotracheal (breathing) tube is used to deliver oxygen and anaesthetic gas to a patient under anaesthesia. In my left hand is one used in humans or large dogs, and in my right is one used in elephants!

Veterinary work is about protecting people as well as animals. In Loiborsoit, Tanzania, in 2016, I took part in a campaign to vaccinate dogs in remote Maasai villages against rabies. The aim was to reduce the incidence of this fatal disease in humans.

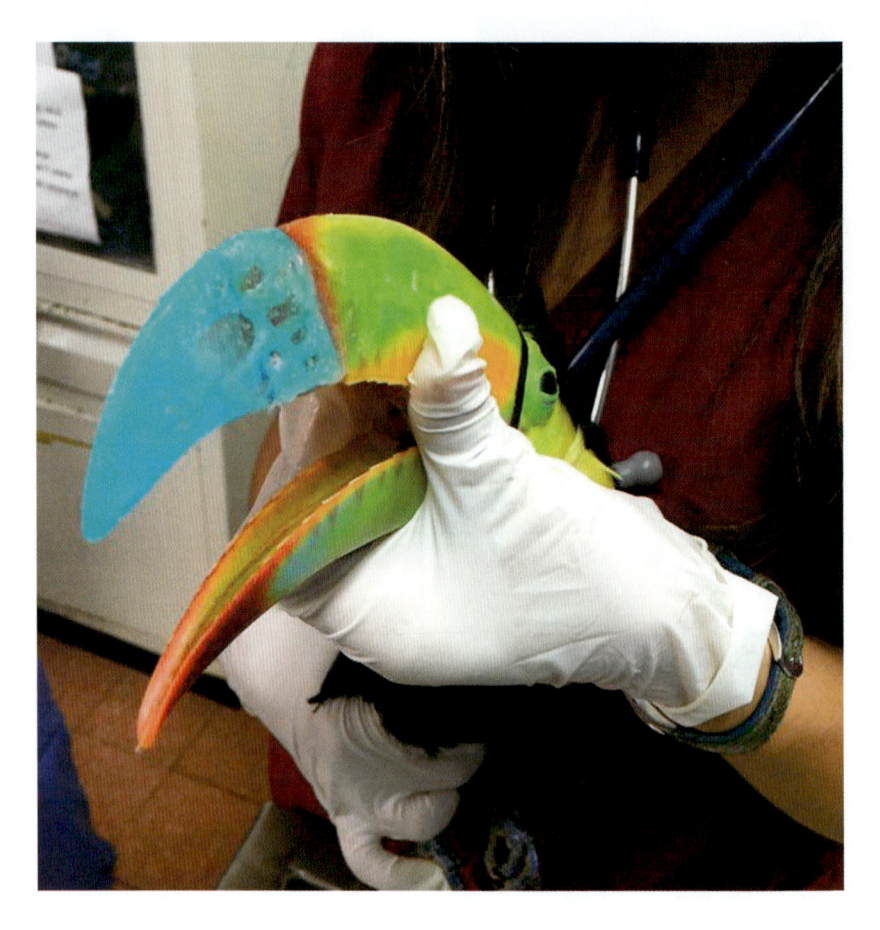

A toucan in Mexico has received a 3D-printed beak after losing part of its own in a suspected wildlife trafficking incident. The patient was confidently using his new prosthesis within hours of its attachment, all thanks to surgeon Dr Beremiz Sanchez!
(Photo source: Dr Beremiz Sanchez)

A harbour seal waiting patiently for her ultrasound to finish.

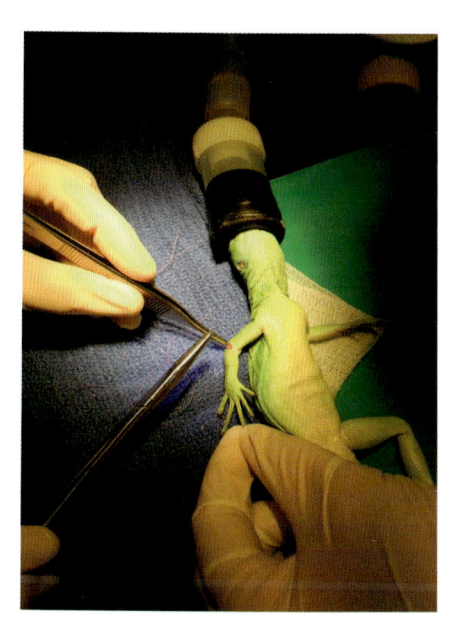

After getting into a fight with its brother, this basilisk lizard came off second best. A quick suture was placed to close the wound, and he was on his way.

This little hedgehog was being seen for inappetence (lack of appetite), which was resolved with medication within a few days.

Visiting a wild population of giant tortoises in the highlands of Santa Cruz Island in the Galapagos archipelago. These animals are one of the longest living of all vertebrates, averaging over 100 years. Some have been known to live closer to 200!

Helping out at a koala hospital after the devastating bushfires of 2020. We found the easiest way to transport them was in washing baskets!

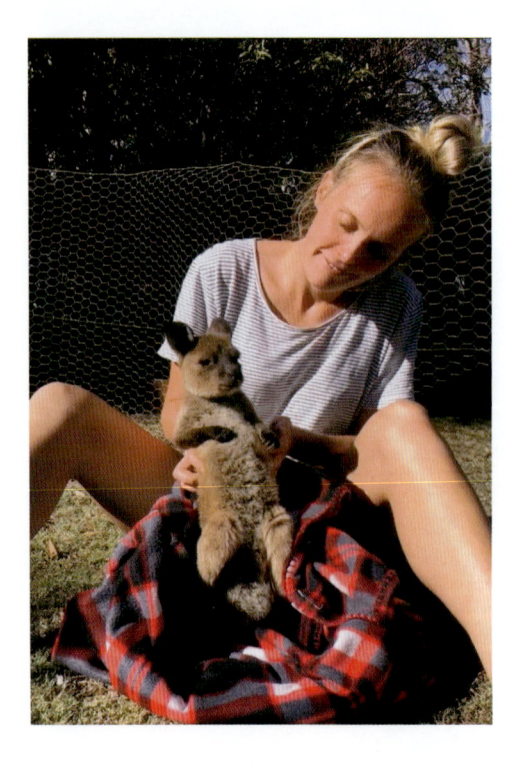

My husband, Jan, and I are currently based on Kangaroo Island, off the coast of South Australia. We enjoy raising orphaned kangaroos when they come into care. This little one is Ruby!

the tiger that was being relocated home to Asia, only to be accidentally flown to Spain instead, which triggered a global hunt for the missing animal. One time, my friend managed to persuade a pilot to leave behind every piece of luggage that was supposed to go into the hold so that there was room on the aircraft for all fifty of his macaque monkeys. That's how important it was that they arrived at their destination together. The passengers, on the other hand, had to wait until the next day for their belongings. Because airlines aren't obligated to disclose when a wild animal is on the flight, chances are that if you ever hear something unusual coming from the undercarriage of your plane, you might have some special cargo on board!

It didn't take me long to settle into my new routine at the Centre. My days would start around five in the morning with the feeding of the hospital's in-patients, which included a jackal that had been injured after being caught in a snare, two servals that had been rescued from the illegal pet trade, two juvenile baboons – both found tied to a pole on the side of the road – and finally, three exceptionally cheeky baby vervet monkeys named Aboo, Affe and, appropriately, Trouble. Just by looking at the vervets, I could tell I had my work cut out for me. Every morning I'd start with their bottle feeds, and it was like working with a group of hyperactive toddlers. Each had its own distinct personality, and collectively they seemed to have a firm idea about how the feeding should be done. Trouble, being the dominant one, needed to be fed first. If I dared to start with anyone else, he'd rip the bottle out of my hand and throw it to the ground in a dramatic tantrum. Meanwhile, Aboo would drink only if he was allowed to hold the bottle himself, which often resulted in more milk going over his body than into his mouth. The solution, I figured out, was to compensate for the spillage by filling his with a little extra. Affe, the smallest and shyest, always came last. He needed a quiet space, away from his boisterous brothers, where he could enjoy his breakfast in silence – something that was suddenly very relatable after just one morning with the group.

Eventually, once they were fed (and Aboo bathed after his milk shower), I'd dash into the jungle at the back of their enclosure to collect some foliage for them to snack on during the day. I say 'dash' in the purest sense of the word: I was acutely aware that Malawi was a country rife with black mamba snakes. If you've never heard of these before, simply know that they're long, fast, aggressive and deadly – a combination I didn't fancy sticking around to see in action. To make matters worse, I'd been told that the US Embassy held the only antivenom treatment in the entire country. Comfortingly, the person who'd pointed this out also highlighted the fact that I'd be dead long before even having time to hail a taxi, so there was really no point in worrying about the logistics of it anyway.

Once I'd made it in and out of the jungle, the next port of call was the jackal. Rather than seeing the animal as menacing, I would think of it as a creature with the body of a dog and the head of a fox, topped with some ridiculously large pointed ears. That made it seem comically cute. He'd been in hospital for three weeks, receiving daily treatment for some nasty wounds that he'd sustained after becoming caught in a snare.

These injuries are all too common, especially in Malawi, where snares are frequently set by people looking for bush meat, or poachers hoping to snag a rhino or elephant. Too often, they also inadvertently trap lions, leopards, cheetahs and wild dogs, and as the animal struggles, the device constricts – typically leading to a slow and painful death. In an attempt to counter this problem, anti-snare collars with built-in studs have been developed. These act to catch the snare around the collar itself, rather than the victim's neck. The collar then sends out a GPS signal, alerting the nearest veterinary team to the animal's whereabouts.

The jackal's story reminded me of a young lion in Tanzania, several years before, which had suffered the same fate. The terrain where the lion lived was such that it was extremely difficult for vets to dart him, therefore making it impossible for them to access him and remove the snare. As he grew bigger, the snare got tighter until, finally, he was too weak to hunt. However, in a true testament to the animal kingdom, his pride kept him alive for an entire three *years* by bringing him food and protecting him until, eventually, a team was able to get there to help.

Since our goal with the jackal was to release him back into the wild, it was imperative during his stay that he didn't become accustomed to humans. To avoid this, all contact was kept to a minimum, and when you *did* have to pay him a visit, you'd do so in a disguise. This meant that on many mornings, after my breakfast routine with the vervets, I'd don a pair of overalls, a hat and a mask before going anywhere near his enclosure. Not only was this an incredibly hot thing to do in a country where the humidity hovers around 1000 per cent, twenty-four hours of the day, but it also severely restricted my ability to move. The mask itself obstructed nearly all of my vision, and there were more than a few occasions when I found myself forward-flipping over the prominent tree roots that lay along the path leading to his enclosure. No doubt the poor jackal was left wondering who the bumbling clown was he'd been stuck with, but we made it through the ordeal together nonetheless. As I delivered his daily medication, I'd always think of the amazing scenes from China, where researchers and veterinarians who work with panda cubs wear entire, head-to-toe panda suits – paws and all – for any interaction with the animals. From having once thought that this was the best work uniform I could imagine, my experiences with the jackal saw me starting to reconsider.

Once the morning routine was done, I'd check in at the hospital to see what procedures, if any, were scheduled for the day. Over the course of the month, this included a fracture repair on one of the servals (which is essentially a spotted cat with legs so long that they may as well be stilts), a call-out to an injured hyena that took no fewer than four evening stake-outs to catch, and a blood draw on a sick African rock python. For anyone whose snake knowledge is as limited as mine, all that needs to be known here is that they can reach up to 4 or *5 metres* in length. Consequently, a task that would normally require two people actually needed twelve; it was certainly no small undertaking.

Between the python, the vervets, the jackal, the hyena hunt, and remaining on the lookout for black mambas in the jungle, I'd use whatever free time I had at the Centre to wander past Simba and Bella's enclosure. I'd sit there with them, enjoying the sunshine, happy that they were now free to spend their lives doing as they pleased. Without fail, I'd find them sitting side by side in some section of bush, except for the moments that Simba would decide to stretch his legs and go for a walk. From the way he moved, I could tell he was riddled with arthritis from his years of confinement and abuse. Over the duration of my stay, I noticed he was having more and more trouble with it. The difficulty he had getting to his feet, the stiffness in his walk, his weight loss – his condition was deteriorating in front of my eyes. His bones were now more prominent than ever, and his skin was starting to hang loosely, slowly falling away from his frame.

At Simba's previous health check, several months earlier, there'd been no cause for concern, other than a slight drop in his kidney function, which could have been explained by the long-term anti-inflammatory medicine he was on to manage his pain. At the time of the health check, there'd been some discussion about altering this medication. Being in Malawi, however, the choices are slim – even more so if you're a lion. In light of Simba's decline in health, we looked into the options once again and managed to find an alternative that could just do the trick. It was gentler on the kidneys but still able to provide adequate pain relief for his condition. With any luck, it might prove to be exactly what he needed. The drug, called Tramadol, was once used widely in both human and veterinary medicine but now tends to be highly restricted because of its potency. Not in Malawi, though, where it was available over the counter, like paracetamol. It turns out that when you're in one of the poorest countries in the world and in desperate need of pain medication for your arthritic lion, you go to the human pharmacy.

As vets, we often visit pharmacies when we're unable to get specific drugs through our own hospitals, so this wasn't a complete surprise to me. It was, however, to the pharmacist. I'll never forget the look on his face when I told him why I needed the Tramadol, or more specifically, who I needed it for. I'm sure he thought I was pulling his leg as I explained that it was for a 200-kilogram lion named Simba. Even with photos, he was dubious at best. Before I could go into how much I'd be needing, the questions started coming thick and fast. 'But how do you medicate him? What's wrong with him? Do the pills make him nauseous? What did you treat him with before? Is he friendly? Can I come and see?' His eyes grew wider and wider as I fielded the questions, and about twenty minutes later, I came away with the Tramadol and an absolute certainty that he hadn't believed a single word I'd said.

Back at the sanctuary, preparations were underway for Simba's anaesthetic. Since we'd made the decision to transition his medication, we had to do an assessment and blood test before that could take place. To answer the pharmacist's question, yes, Simba was friendly, but still I wouldn't be going anywhere near him unless he was well and truly asleep. A general anaesthetic was required for this, so we prepared all the drugs, darts and equipment, ready for the procedure the following morning. The supplies available to us were limited, so we had to make do with what we had. Instead of a face mask to deliver the oxygen, I'd cut a hole in an empty margarine container through which I could attach the tubing. Instead of an X-ray machine, we had to rely on our skills of palpation to assess any questionable areas of his body. Instead of floor scales, we'd have to find a way to suspend him from a spring balance on the roof to record his weight. And, instead of being able to transport him into our clinic, we'd be doing all of this inside his den.

It was shortly after dawn when we gathered outside the enclosure with our equipment in tow, margarine container and all. I'd carried the oxygen tank, acutely aware that if I were to trip over a tree root while holding it, I'd create a solid metal rocket. This container of pressurised gas had only a small red cap at the top securing all the contents. Should the cap be knocked off, you'll have instantly created a torpedo that's capable of blasting through a solid brick wall at close to 100 kilometres an hour. *Surely, what we were doing was an accident waiting to happen*, I thought. There was a reason that the tank had been designed to stay in one place. Usually, this place is chained to the wall of a hospital. Instead, we were carrying ours through a jungle! On arrival, I took tremendous care in putting down the tank and permanently relinquishing my duties with it.

In a morning that could only get easier from here, we swiftly proceeded to separate the two lions, both of whom were grumbling – clearly displeased about having been fasted the night before. When Simba was alone, the grumbling escalated into full-blown, eardrum-rupturing roaring once he'd caught sight of our blow dart. We wasted no time in darting him, then waited in silence for the drugs to take effect, tentatively opening the door and entering the enclosure at the ten-minute mark. I gently prodded Simba with a stick, ready to fly out the door if he so much as moved a whisker. He didn't. The coast was clear to start our work, which took a little under thirty minutes.

First was the blood draw, which was taken from the large vein running up his front leg. Holding Simba's paw, squeezing it gently to encourage the blood flow required both my hands, the sheer size of him simply awe-inspiring in every way. In saying that, he was a shadow of his former self. His weight loss was even more apparent as he lay there, his hips and ribs dramatically protruding from under his coat. I opened his mouth to check his teeth, suspecting that the weight loss was due to his declining kidney function, but wanting to ensure that we weren't missing any dental disease in the process. We weren't. It wasn't a good sign for the ageing lion, nor was the bony mass I could palpate on his hip. Without an X-ray, we'd be unable to reach a definitive diagnosis, but the overwhelming probability was that it was cancer. In a cat of Simba's age, presenting with the signs he had, it was almost certain. At least it offered an additional explanation for his dramatic weight loss, and given these findings, we made the decision to finish the rest of our examination promptly.

Simba recovered smoothly from his anaesthetic, and I remained with him for the rest of the day for observation. When the blood test returned from the laboratory, it showed that his kidney function hadn't deteriorated from the reading that was taken several months before. It did, however, support the growing concerns of cancer. Simba would receive palliative care until it was deemed that his suffering was too great. For the time being, his life with Bella was a happy one, and he was still able to do all the things that a lion should. Once he was transitioned onto Tramadol, there was a vast improvement to his mobility almost instantly.

It was a bittersweet ending to my dealings with Simba. I did draw comfort from the knowledge that he was in good hands.

As my stay in Malawi came to a close, I made a point of returning to the pharmacist. I wanted to show him some photos of the lion he'd helped, and with any luck, he might just believe me this time. If I thought his eyes had been wide with astonishment in our last meeting, it was nothing compared to this one. It was incredible to see the awe on his face, and the smile that appeared in knowing he'd made a difference in the life of an animal as special as Simba. I thanked him and left with the certainty that Simba would remain one of his most unique and memorable patients, just as he would mine.

Before arriving in Malawi, I'd had no idea what an impact this visit would have on me. I certainly hadn't anticipated meeting Simba. A couple of years later, I had an opportunity to meet the president of Born Free, Will Travers OBE, in London, and tell him about my time with the lion that his organisation had helped rescue. The entire experience was a formative one for me. Subsequently, I have redirected my focus towards supporting the smaller-scale institutions that do important work despite having limited means. The Lilongwe Wildlife Centre is a perfect example of this, although there are countless others around the world that care for animals rescued from harrowing circumstances.

Knowing that Simba had been saved from horrors to live out his days in peace brought me a deep happiness. With it came a profound gratitude for all involved. Countless people worked together to give him a better life, and in return, I suspect they got from it a massive sense of fulfilment. The co-founder of the Born Free organisation, actress (and star of movies including *A Town Like Alice* and *Born Free*) Virginia McKenna, puts it this way: 'People are increasingly aware of how wild animals can be exploited and can suffer, and perhaps long to be a part of a caring and positive story.' That has certainly been true for me.

10
South Africa

AS OUR UNNERVINGLY small plane bumped and pitched its way into the airport at Mbombela, I'd reached my final African destination for the year. In the space of a short forty-five-minute flight from the South African city of Johannesburg, I'd gone from a bustling mega-city to the wilderness in its truest form. As we came in to land, I could see mountains and cliff faces rising out of the bushland below, revealing themselves through the morning mist. What a perfect place it was to be ending my African adventure. Well, for now at least.

It was here, on the outskirts of the famous Kruger National Park – only an hour west from the border with Mozambique – that I'd be spending a month learning about what everyday life is like as a wildlife vet in South

Africa. I'd be shadowing accomplished veterinarians in their daily work to get a better understanding of what, exactly, it meant to be a practising veterinarian out here. Already, it was hard to believe how much I'd been able to see and do in such a short period on this vast continent. The range of experiences I'd had in this time seemed to reflect the incredible diversity of a place I'd come to love. I had no idea where the rest of this adventure would take me, but I was looking forward to finding out.

There were two main reasons I'd chosen South Africa as my last stop on the continent. Firstly, it's no secret that working in Africa, South Africa in particular, is the dream of many young and aspiring wildlife veterinarians and conservationists. It's unlike anywhere else in the world. In among the beauty of the plains, jungles, savannas, mountains and wildlife for which it's known are the challenges that come with being a nation struggling with the desperation of poverty and conflict. For this reason, the wildlife of South Africa is under persistent threat of decimation at the hands of poachers. As a consequence, the country has also developed into a hub of veterinary activity.

That brings me to my other reason for wanting to come here: to assist and learn from the veterinarians who work on the frontline of this onslaught. Over the past decade, South Africa has become a poaching battlefield, and my next location, Kruger National Park, was a leading hotspot. This is a relatively new development; in its heyday of the 1990s and early 2000s, the park was recognised for its dense population of wildlife. But what was once home to over 80 per cent of the world's rhino population, and regarded as a safe haven, with fewer than twenty poaching attempts a year, has now become one of the most dangerous places on earth for these animals. The incidence of rhino poaching has exploded so dramatically here in recent years that the number of slaughtered animals rose from just thirteen in 2007, to over 800 in 2015. And that's only within the park itself.

This staggering increase in poaching activity can be explained by several factors. First and foremost, poachers tend to go where the defences are weaker and there are more animals to annihilate. In the past, this has seen countries like Zimbabwe, Congo, Sudan, Gabon and Mozambique take the brunt of it, but as their wildlife populations dwindled, the poachers have moved south into new territories. In addition, the recent introduction of tightened laws and penalties for poaching in East Africa has reduced poaching rates by up to 90 per cent in these regions and forced poachers to look for easier pickings. These factors, coupled with the rising value of ivory and rhino horns – fuelled by an insatiable demand from the Chinese and Vietnamese markets – have seen a perfect storm of poaching activity erupt in southern Africa, a storm that has centred itself right over Kruger National Park. What has since transpired, thanks in part to the massive profitability of this industry, is the emergence of sophisticated poaching syndicates and crime cartels that have begun coordinating highly organised attacks in the area to meet the demand. And because of the geographical arrangement of the park – it shares an extensive border with Mozambique, one of Africa's most impoverished nations – the poachers' access to the animals is proving all too easy.

For the better part of the next month, I'd be living on the outskirts of Kruger, on a farm just outside the large town of Mbombela, nestled in the foothills of a spectacular mountain range that spans the entire length of the country. On-site was a small veterinary clinic with a live-in veterinarian, as well as a team of vets who provided wildlife capture and translocation services to the surrounding community and its reserves. It was this team that I'd be spending the majority of my time with, and over the coming month we'd be responding together to call-outs all over the north-eastern corner of the country.

The property I was staying on was simply enormous, spanning as far as the eye could see in every direction. Being at the foothills of the mountains, the land was gently sloping and littered with boulders and shrubs. Its elevation provided a magnificent view of the surrounding landscape from just about every vantage point. There was an abundance of wildlife that called this place home, and driving up the steep, dirt driveway was often an exercise in patience while you waited for some ambling giraffes or zebras to pass by at their leisure. I was staying about halfway up the property, in a small boma that was not too dissimilar from my one in Zimbabwe. The difference was that here there were no other buildings within eyeshot, and from my bed I had a sweeping view out over the plains below. Every morning I'd wake to the sound of zebras munching loudly on their morning meal, and monkeys thundering across my thatched roof – no doubt plotting which one of my shoes they'd pinch that day.

My time was well divided between the capture work itself and assisting the on-site vet with the hospital in-patients. Unsurprisingly, due to our location, many of the captures were in response to rhino poaching attempts, or to move an animal out of harm's way. It was not uncommon to attend a call-out at about five in the morning and to return to base only in the early hours of the evening. The work was confronting, physically demanding and intense, and soon I began to get an appreciation of how much of a toll it can take – on both your body and emotions. Between these call-outs, there were also plenty of rogue elephants to keep us busy, giraffes that had been trapped in snares by people looking for bush meat, and even some leopards that had suffered the same fate.

When not out tending to a rhino, elephant or giraffe – as the vast majority of my days were shaping up to be – I'd be back at the farm, attending instead to the hospital's in-patients. For the first two weeks of my stay, this would include a pool of sickly crocodiles and an ostrich named Eric, who arrived three days after me. The crocodiles and I didn't develop an instant rapport (nor did we develop one down the track, either, for that matter), but Eric and I did. In fact, he remains one of my fondest memories from my time in South Africa.

The capture team had received a report from a member of the public about a weak and emaciated ostrich lying by the side of the road on a nearby reserve and had retrieved him. Eric was carried in on a stretcher – not unlike how a human patient might be delivered, but a lot more feathery. He was an absolute mess – he was covered in dirt, his eyes were firmly closed, his skin hung loosely from his frame and his body was riddled with ticks. His long, slender form lay limp, and he allowed us to get to work without putting up any form of resistance, which is never a good sign from a wild animal. This is particularly true of any avian species, which are widely known – and feared – in the veterinary world for masking illness until they're well and truly at death's door.

Quickly, I took a sample of blood from the large vein running along Eric's neck, and found another vein on the inside of his leg to place a catheter in. We administered fluids to correct his dehydration while also running tests to work out what might have happened to him. Immediately, our suspicions were firmly in one of two camps. He was either suffering from a severe parasitic infection or he'd ingested something he shouldn't have. My money was on the latter, as ostriches are notorious for swallowing anything that looks interesting, which, for an ostrich, is everything. Should this happen, it's more often than not that the object will become lodged in their digestive tract, eventually stopping the animal from wanting to eat and sending them on a downhill trajectory. Unfortunately, to confirm such a thing would require an X-ray, something that we couldn't provide. Instead, after the parasite exam had come back negative, we made the decision to manage him with supportive care and see how he responded.

After spending two nights in hospital regaining some of his strength, Eric was placed outside in a hospital boma where we could continue to closely monitor him. It was around this time I learned that his 'supportive care' would involve me forcibly feeding him at least twice a day. This was less of an issue while he was still feeling under the weather, but as the days went by, it quickly became one. The problem – for me, at least – began to arise as his strength returned and he decided that he no longer wanted to actively participate in these sessions, which involved me passing a tube down his exceptionally long throat. Little did he know, I'd have also preferred not to be doing it, but unfortunately for the both of us it was necessary for his recovery. So, regardless of what was scheduled for the day on the farm, my days – for weeks on end – would start and finish with a visit to Eric's boma.

In a short space of time I went from having a bare-minimum knowledge of ostriches to knowing far more than I ever could have hoped or wished. I feared that my newfound knowledge was nothing more than a collection of highly obscure and useless facts, but they were the things that helped me get through this experience nonetheless. To start, a general rule of thumb is that the redder the legs, the angrier the ostrich. Eric was a placid bird, but even the gentlest of animals can get quickly fed up with having a tube put down their throat multiple times a day. When his legs were turning scarlet, I knew he needed a moment. Then, once we'd passed that hurdle, it was all about the approach. In my experience, ostriches can go from zero to sixty in the space of a second, and if you startle them, they can go headlong into either you or a wall at top speed – causing monumental damage to both. To avoid this element of surprise, it's best to approach them slowly and from the side, and it doesn't hurt to pretend you're really not interested in them at all. Even better, if you have a stick with a shiny object on it, dangle it in front of them and soon they'll have forgotten about you entirely (the key here is to make sure they don't eat it, or you're back to square one).

By now, it's time for the final step in an ostrich capture, which is the part where you have to quickly embrace the nearly 2-metre-tall, 100-kilogram bird in a big bear hug. Unless you are a professional basketball player, there is a good chance that it will be towering over you at this stage, and going in for the hug takes a fair amount of pluck. If you are lucky, though, the bird will be so distracted by the shiny object that it won't have noticed you until your arms are securely around it. Once in the hug, with downward pressure applied to the wings, the ostrich becomes quite amenable – no doubt realising that the jig is up. From here, it's surprisingly little trouble to gently pull the neck down to your height and insert the feeding tube into its throat to deliver the meal. And voilà – that was how Eric and I occupied ourselves, morning and night, for weeks on end.

Between our slew of call-outs, my daily dance routine with Eric, and trying my best to avoid the hospital crocs, the days blurred into weeks and the weeks soon became a month. There are, however, a few encounters that remain foremost in my mind, and one of these was the day I met Aleks.

It was close to lunchtime one day, about halfway into my stay on the farm. I'd just returned from feeding Eric, and planned to visit the clinic to see if we'd had any new arrivals that morning. The short walk through the scrub from my boma took me along a well-worn dirt track, eroded from the hundreds of hooves that had pounded their way through this grassland on a daily basis. On arrival at the clinic, I discovered that the team had been called out to a rogue elephant that was causing havoc down the road. I was greeted instead by a young European vet who'd come to do a a few weeks of research – Aleks. He was completing a series of medication trials on a new anaesthetic he was hoping to have approved for use in Russia. For this reason, he was here to assist the team with a variety of their captures, and would be using this drug to assess its efficacy. All going well, it could then be licensed for use elsewhere in the world.

As the two of us meandered down to the kitchen to find some lunch, he began to talk about why it was so important to have this drug approved for use in Russia, of all places. Interestingly, Aleks's role was a mixture of wildlife veterinarian, specialist veterinary anaesthetist and professional polar bear mover. What an amazing job title! Soon we were deep in conversation – not one I'd expect to be having in the middle of the South African bush. Aleks told met he was responsible for the safe capture and translocation of wild polar bears in northern Russia each year. The project – nicknamed the 'Air Bear Mission' – was one I'd never heard of, and I couldn't quite decide if I was more taken with the name of it or the image of a polar bear strapped to the skids of a helicopter in the middle of the Arctic Circle. Before I could ask why such a thing was necessary, he proceeded to explain that much of his work was linked to the changing climate. Specifically, the ice the bears would normally hunt on has begun to melt in recent years, forcing them inland towards villages and townships in search of food. To avoid risk to the people, Aleks would arrange for the annual translocation of the bears, by helicopter, from the outskirts of these remote Russian settlements to an area where they could safely hunt without causing trouble or harm to those around them. Since very few capture drugs were approved for use in Russia, he needed the approval of this one for his work to continue – and that was what had brought him here.

By this stage, I found myself oscillating between feelings of awe and dread. *Please don't let there be a lull in the conversation*, I thought. If forced to try to contribute something, I had nothing even remotely as fascinating as what he'd just told me. My daily tango with Eric wouldn't make the cut, I was certain of that. Thankfully, no interjection from me was required. Aleks went on to say he'd be using the drug first thing the next morning on a herd of blesbok, a flighty type of antelope, that needed translocating. A nearby capture team, he added, was scheduled to move a herd of zebras at the same time. On hearing this, I was over the moon, as group captures were something I'd come here to learn about in particular. The approach differs drastically from the way a single animal is captured, and I was looking forward to finding out more about it.

That evening, I met with the zebra capture team to discuss our strategy. The herd we planned to move was located on a private reserve, near the southern aspect of Kruger National Park. An overabundance of grazing animals there was putting too much pressure on the food supply, so the plan was to translocate the zebras to a neighbouring property. In the process, we'd also be taking blood samples from each animal for routine disease surveillance. Unlike a single animal, which can be easily darted or trapped (or even caught using a net gun from a helicopter), herd animals are usually captured and moved as an entire group. As a consequence, specific *physical* capture techniques are used. For the zebras, I discovered, we'd be using what's known as a 'plastic boma' technique, perhaps best described as an elaborate series of curtains that are assembled in the middle of the bush. The entire setup is a giant triangular structure – about 130 metres wide at the opening, extending about 350 metres deep – with two large plastic sheets running along the outside as the 'walls'. Inside these walls is the series of curtains, and these get closer together the deeper you go into the boma, creating an enclosed funnel system in which to trap the animals. Two teams – one in the air and one on land – are required to operate this system. The helicopter team finds and directs the herd into the wide opening of the boma, while the ground team hides within the folds of the curtain sheets. Once the alarm sounds from the helicopter, signalling that the herd has entered the boma, those on the curtains run to close them – trapping the herd deeper and deeper within the structure as they go.

Catching a herd of running zebras (or running anything, for that matter) is a complex task with a bewildering number of moving parts. It's also something that requires a thorough understanding of the species being handled.

As zebras are prone to stress, aggression and injury, all precautions must be taken to minimise risks. For the helicopter team, it was crucial to ensure that herds or family groups weren't mixed together when directing the animals into the boma, as that was a sure-fire way for utter chaos to erupt among this socially selective species. We were told that, should a zebra suddenly find itself in an enclosed area with other zebras it doesn't know, the only way to prevent World War Three from happening would be to hastily cut a hole in the plastic wall and let the entire lot of them out.

For those of us on the ground, on the other hand, it was our job to take special care when *handling* the animals. Specifically, that meant ensuring that we didn't make eye contact with the zebras. As is the case for any prey species, looking these animals directly in the eye can be perceived as a threat and cause an instant and massive amount of adrenaline release. When in an already highly stressful environment – such as a capture scenario – this adrenaline release can be enough to cause catastrophic damage to the heart muscle in a process known as capture myopathy. In extreme cases, it can even lead to death.

Interestingly, while capture myopathy has been studied and documented in veterinary literature for the past fifty years, it was only in the 2000s that a syndrome remarkably similar to it began to appear in human medical literature. It was called 'takotsubo cardiomyopathy', also known as broken heart syndrome, and what was interesting about it was that people were presenting with the classic signs of a heart attack but had no evidence of such on any tests. On further examination, these individuals with broken heart syndrome were exhibiting the same changes to the muscle wall that were being seen in the veterinary world in animals with capture myopathy. Perhaps the most fascinating part of it all, though, was what the patients had in common. What seemed to link them was a recent event of severe emotional stress – seeing a loved one pass away, going through a divorce, or losing everything in a natural disaster, to name a few. It was an important discovery in the human medical world, as it appeared to confirm the powerful connection between heart and mind – offering evidence that intense, painful emotions in the brain can set off alarming, life-threatening physical changes in the heart, exactly as we see in animals.

With all of this in mind, and my role as one of the 'curtain runners' firmly established, I was quietly apprehensive about how the capture would play out. In what seemed like the blink of an eye, the morning arrived and the time for misgivings had passed. Instead, by barely seven in the morning, I was filled with dread for an altogether different reason. It had been drummed into us that, for this capture, it was important to dress in camouflage or at least in 'bush' colours. Much of today's success would hinge on whether those of us on the ground could effectively hide in the curtain sheets and not alert the animals to our presence until they were already in the trap. A quick scan of my washing that day revealed that the only T-shirt available to me was a black-and-white striped one. Yes, black-and-white stripes: what a faux pas! Given that I did have a pair of khaki pants, surely it was really only *half* a faux pas, I consoled myself.

Around half past seven, we arrived at the capture site. The plastic boma had been assembled overnight and it was nothing short of enormous. There were about five series of curtains, and I took my position on the second row, one in from the opening. There were three of us responsible for closing this particular curtain, which would involve dragging it about 100 metres, as fast as we could, to the other side. We hid inside the folds and waited in total silence for the signal from above. Being unable to see anything yet able to hear the helicopters circling overhead and feel the thunder of hooves reverberating through the ground as the herd approached was a surreal experience.

Suddenly, there was a rush of action and a deafening noise as the first alarm sounded, the signal for the team on the first curtain to run and close their 'gate'. I knew this meant that the zebras were now inside the boma with us and braced myself for what was to come. I don't think anything could have prepared me for the adrenaline surge of the moment when the fifty-strong herd of wild zebras tore past our hiding spot. Their size, speed and power hit me like a tonne of bricks – especially when finding myself within an arm's length of them in a tightly enclosed space. The alarm sounded again from above, signalling for those of us on the second curtain to run. In a fraction of a second, we dived out of the curtain and sprinted as fast as we could to the other side of the opening, frantically dragging our enormous piece of plastic with us.

As I was about halfway across the clearing with the curtain billowing out behind me, the zebras seemed to figure out they'd been driven into a trap. It was bedlam as the animals started hurling themselves in every direction, moving erratically and violently in an attempt to get out. Visibility had reduced to almost nothing, thanks to the combined action of the helicopter and hooves kicking up dust from every angle. It was getting difficult to even know which way was up. During this time of madness, it seemed ludicrous that the only thing separating this frantic herd from the outside world was us and a flimsy plastic sheet. They seemed to have decided they wanted out, so …

Scarcely had I registered that thought when the helicopters chased the zebras deeper into the boma and the signal was sounding once more for the team on curtain number three.

Once all the curtains were shut and the herd was trapped inside the small, narrow enclosure at the end of our boma, the animals were darted individually with sedative. This was done to ensure the safe collection of their blood samples, and subsequent movement of the animals onto the trucks. We'd elected to capture this herd in two stages because of its size, and having just successfully completed part one, I was beginning to feel more confident about the second lot.

This confidence proved to be fleeting, as right then the unthinkable happened. I was bending down to take a blood sample from the first zebra when, in a fraction of a second, my pants ripped from top to bottom. Right down the middle. My underwear was on show to not only the fifty zebras I was sitting in the middle of, but also the almost twenty people I was working with. It seemed my misgivings about the day were coming to fruition. So much for restoring my reputation after turning up to the capture in a questionable outfit. Fortunately (or unfortunately, as it soon turned out to be), one of my colleagues happened to have a spare pair of pants in the car. But then – as if this was one of those nightmares you're unable to wake up from – it turned out that these pants were a pair of black-and-white pinstriped shorts. Before I had a chance to ask why someone even owns shorts like that, let alone why they'd bring them to a capture, I quickly reminded myself that people in glass houses weren't in a position to throw stones. Swallowing my pride, I accepted the offer and, after a quick change, there I was in the middle of the African bush, out on a zebra capture dressed head-to-toe as a zebra myself. If I'd thought that the rhino incident was a low point in my career, or perhaps even that regrettable experience with the ophthalmic exam back in veterinary school, I was wrong. This was, by far, the new winner.

In what shaped up to be one of the longest days of my life, we managed to complete the second zebra capture reasonably smoothly. Other than, of course, the relentless ribbing I was subjected to about my personal spin on bush wear and camouflage. It was surprising we managed to get anything done given how much this banter came to dominate the rest of the day's proceedings. At one stage, it was even suggested that I was bound to have more luck than anyone else capturing the zebras, seeing how easily I could be mistaken for one of their own. This was far from the case, I can assure you.

My outfit brought me no concessions from the herd of antelope we captured that afternoon. Originally, they'd been scheduled for relocation the following day but when we found we had extra time up our sleeves, we did it there and then.

This capture worked much the same way it did for the zebras, except that we had to refashion the final section of the funnel into a netted enclosure. Unlike the plastic walls, this netting would provide a softer landing area for this flighty and excitable species. Known for jumping almost as frequently as it runs, the impala is a medium-sized, slender antelope with long, fine legs, razor-sharp hooves, and dagger-like horns. It spooks easily, and will spring off in any direction when startled, like a four-legged jack-in-the-box. For this reason, the netting was there to catch and entangle the impalas before they could do any serious damage to themselves, or possibly even *our*selves.

This time we were positioned in the final section of the boma, in and around the netting that – all things going well – our targets would soon be landing on. We were equipped with an unusual combination of tools: syringes full of sedatives and a handful of pool noodles. Following instructions, we hid in the scrubs and bushes within this section of the enclosure and took care to find reasonable shelter that might protect us from any airborne impalas landing on our heads. With a limited briefing on exactly what to expect, all I knew was to be ready to either snatch one out of the sky as it flew overhead, or quickly untangle it from the netting behind me.

As the helicopter team chased the herd into our trap, we remained hidden and waited for the siren that would alert us that the entrance to the boma had been closed. If I thought that all hell had broken loose on the zebra capture, I was wrong. It was as if we'd taken the zebras and given them wings. There were impalas flinging and springing in every direction – both on the ground and above it – and the best you could do was to brace for impact. I took cover as the siren sounded, watching the commotion unfold above, waiting and hoping that they'd find their way into the netting so I'd have the slightest chance of catching one. In the flurry of action and the panic of the moment, I grabbed the closest thing I could see as a form of defence against the hundred-strong herd, which happened to be a small twig from the bush I was sheltering under. Any reasonable person would have realised how fruitless and ridiculous such a thing was and quickly desisted. I did it anyway.

Within seconds, and with no help whatsoever from my twig, our impalas were entangled in the netting and we scrambled to pull them out. We immediately injected each animal with a sedative and blindfolded them to reduce stress. One by one, we hoisted the sedated animals onto our shoulders and carried them directly to the waiting truck, and within ten minutes they were all loaded and ready to go. The last step in the process was to take the pool noodles and slip them over the horns to reduce the chance of them injuring themselves in transit.

As the zebras and impalas made their journey north, we made ours back to the farm. Having come to South Africa with the hope of participating in a group capture, there was no doubt I'd got what I'd come for, even if I *had* managed to thoroughly embarrass myself in the process. Given what I'd just gone through, I was almost thankful that I had only a few days remaining on the continent, as it surely meant there was a limit to how many more mortifying situations I could manoeuvre myself into.

I am pleased to report that the final few days went down without a hitch, although they were as action-packed as the last handful of months had been. The last weekend, in fact, began with a situation so heartbreaking that I longed to be back – loud and proud – in my zebra suit.

Overnight we'd received a report of a rhino poaching on a reserve down the road from us. We hurried to the site to find a female white rhino that had been shot, but was still alive by the time we arrived. She hadn't had her horn harvested, leading us to the conclusion that the poachers had been interrupted. Thankfully, she didn't appear to have a calf, as the young typically stay by their mother's side, which makes the young rhinos vulnerable to being attacked themselves – be it shot, stabbed or struck with a machete – as they are known for causing interference to the poacher's work by doing all they can to defend their mother. For those that survive, the trauma is clear. When found, they are often vocalising, or crying, close to their mother, and take months to physically and emotionally recover in the care of one of the many rhino orphanages around South Africa. Social interactions are important for this species, and for these orphans, one of the most significant parts of their recovery is the friendship found in the fellow orphans with which they now share their lives.

One of the vets I was with instantly recognised the rhino. She'd been attacked before. The bullets used to shoot her had missed her vital organs, yet forensic tests had been unable to trace them back to the offending parties. I couldn't bear to imagine what she'd been through in her life, although her story was far from unique. In fact, she could almost be considered one of the lucky ones, in what is a truly horrendous thing to think about. Most of them, after all, are too badly injured to be saved, and have to be euthanised straightaway. Probably the most horrific of these instances is when the poachers haven't used a gun or sedative to immobilise the animal, but have instead taken a machete to the spine – leaving the animal conscious throughout the attack, yet paralysed so it's unable to flee. For the ones that can be saved, on the other hand, the road to recovery is extremely long and difficult. These animals require extensive treatment in hospital, and often must undergo repeated reconstructive facial surgeries to close the gaping wounds left behind from the attack.

We immediately provided the injured rhino with sedation and pain relief. The bullet entry point was just above her shoulder, thankfully far away from any vital structures. An X-ray would be needed to confirm if there were any others within her head, chest or abdomen, and a team of veterinarians from the national park had been called to assist with this. We started by administering emergency fluids into several of her veins. This was critical if we were to prevent her from going into kidney failure as a consequence of the potentially lengthy period of time she'd been lying on her side: we had no idea how long she'd been there so we erred on the side of caution. The sheer weight of her body in this position could be enough to crush her own muscles, releasing a toxic protein into her blood. It would take hours of these fluids to flush out the protein before we'd even be able to get her to stand. The worry was that if she stood up too early, the massive amount of protein released in her bloodstream would be fatal.

Once she was sufficiently stabilised, we made the decision to remove her horn ourselves. Dehorning, as it's known, is now a common procedure that's undertaken throughout Africa in a desperate bid to protect the animals from attack. The thought process behind it is to physically remove the bounty that's on the animal's head, although the decision to do so is never undertaken lightly. These animals still require around-the-clock supervision to safeguard against attack, as dehorned rhinos have still been known to be poached in revenge. They may also be attacked simply so the poachers can recover the minuscule amount of horn tissue left behind at the base of the skull – proving how desperate these people are to get their hands on even the smallest amount of the stuff.

The dehorning procedure was carried out swiftly while our patient was still under heavy sedation. The horn itself is akin to our fingernails. It's made of exactly the same stuff – keratin: it regrows when cut and has no pain receptors, making trimming or cutting it pain-free – until you accidentally (or intentionally) hit the underlying tissue or skin. The demand for rhino horn is driven by the false belief that it holds magical, medicinal properties. By that logic, our toenail clippings should hold magical, medicinal properties, too. The devastation caused by harvesting horn is senseless.

When the team from the national park finally arrived, we handed the care of the rhino over to them. They'd stay with her, continuing to administer the fluids, until she was able to stand. They'd also assess her for further bullet injuries, and then transfer her to hospital, where she'd begin her treatment and rehabilitation. At this stage, it was imperative for us to get the horn to the secure and secret location where, by law, it must be stored.

Veterinarians performing dehornings are almost always accompanied by an armed guard, for good reason. Now, finding ourselves in possession of a horn without such protection, we felt vulnerable. It was in everybody's best interests to get it out of our hands as quickly as possible.

The ride to Pretoria was tense. Our usually talkative and animated group sat in silence as we sped through the city streets, tearing through the traffic, barely stopping at red lights. Everyone was looking out for the gates of the facility that was our destination. At last, we could see them in the distance, and there was a collective sucking in of breath. Everyone was aware of the danger of what we were doing. Although our 'harvest' consisted of only 800 grams of horn, it was worth about US$50,000, and in the eyes of some people, this was easily enough to kill for.

To reduce the risk of ambush on arrival, we called ahead to arrange for the people at the facility to open the gates as they saw us approach. Sure we'd set a new land speed record for a journey between Greater Kruger and Pretoria, we safely deposited the horn. There were sighs of relief all round.

I was still reeling from the morning's activities – an experience that would stay with me for many years to come. Now was not the time to reflect on it, however, because while we were in Pretoria, the veterinarian I was accompanying suggested we pay a visit to the local zoo. A week earlier, she'd received a call about one of their animals and wanted to use this opportunity to investigate.

At the zoo, I saw the final two cases of my African adventure, neither of which was anything I could have ever anticipated. If anything, they were probably two of the most unusual cases I'd come across on the continent.

The first was a tiger with a suspected sore tooth, the tooth being less of an issue than the species. Tigers occur naturally in Asia and were certainly not an animal I'd expected to find myself working with in this part of the world. The second patient was a lioness that had mysteriously morphed into a lion by growing a mane. While this was more predictable geographically, nothing else about the case seemed typical.

As we entered the zoo, I was struck by its beauty. It was just after nine in the morning – although, considering how much we'd already packed into the day, it felt like it should have been nine in the evening – and for the most part, we had it all to ourselves. The zoo was situated on a large, sloping hill, with lush and leafy grounds. A variety of animals were visible through the trees. The buildings, though old, were grand and their elaborate architecture was slightly worn from more than a hundred years of use. It seemed strange to be in Africa, a place known for its wild, natural beauty and free-roaming animals, yet standing in a zoo. However, for many people living on this continent, a zoo is the only place they'd ever have a chance of seeing these creatures for themselves.

One of the zoo's vets met us near the entrance and took us into the hospital to explain the day's proceedings. It became obvious that the reason we'd been called was to investigate the possibility of using Aleks's new anaesthetic on the tiger with the toothache. There were pluses and minuses to weigh up. It was being hailed as a safer alternative to some of the existing anaesthetics. This was particularly true for geriatric patients, and, at fifteen years old, our tiger certainly was approaching that category. The downside to the drug was an unusual phenomenon documented in big cats. If I tell you the phenomenon was called 'spontaneous awakenings', I'm sure you'll appreciate this was something anyone would rather avoid. The prospect of it happening on my watch didn't thrill me: I was about to spend an hour with a stripy, dagger-toothed creature that, should it awaken, looked like it could almost swallow me whole.

Aleks's explanation that these spontaneous awakenings occurred in response to movement helped settle the matter. Provided we took care not to change the position of the animal once anaesthetised, he said, there shouldn't be any problem. But then he added a poorly timed anecdote about a veterinarian in America who was elbow-deep in a tiger's throat, passing down a breathing tube, when the animal suddenly woke up and nearly removed the arm in one go. Somehow, the vet managed to escape with his arm intact, but this story haunted me for the rest of that day and long afterwards, if I'm to be honest.

For the past few weeks, the tiger had been reluctant to eat and had a small swelling on the side of his face that hadn't improved with medication. The plan was to anaesthetise him so that an examination of his mouth could be performed – somehow without movement – and an some blood could be taken for a general health assessment. The procedure was to be performed in the den at the back of the animal's enclosure, rather than in the hospital itself. Given that it was only a quick examination that required limited equipment, there was no need to move him from his living quarters.

As we entered the tiger's den, I laid eyes on him for the first time. A 250-kilogram, 3-metre-long orange mass of muscle, our patient appeared to be reasonably annoyed by our presence. Even worse, he showed no signs of being in his twilight years. Quite the opposite, in fact. He was spritely and agile, and moved about the area with great speed and dexterity. He let out a roar that made all the hairs on the back of my neck stand up and also echoed all the way down the long, narrow hallway we were standing in, making for a frighteningly protracted experience. Gathered in this small space were a handful of zookeepers, two local veterinary students, Aleks, the zoo vet and myself – so the way to the exit was well and truly obstructed if I had any thoughts about making a quick getaway. Quelling that realisation, I turned my attention back to the tiger and waited for Aleks to dart him through the bars.

Ten minutes later, once we were confident that our patient was asleep thanks to the sophisticated prod-him-with-a-broomstick test, we opened the door to the enclosure and tentatively entered. It took about ten of us to hoist him up onto the stretcher – moving him as little as possible, of course – and I didn't enjoy my position at the head. In that moment, I'd have happily traded it to be back on the giraffe's neck. As we lifted the tiger, I noticed that the drug hadn't seemed to eliminate twitching. Since I was already on edge, thanks to Aleks's earlier story, this was an unsettling discovery.

We were quick in collecting our samples. The blood would tell us if he was fit for a longer anaesthetic, which he would have to have if there was indeed something wrong with his tooth. Nothing could be seen on examination of his mouth, and we couldn't do an X-ray of the jaw to confirm that he was suffering from one of the most commonly seen oral complaints – a tooth root infection. To treat such a thing would require an extraction of the affected tooth or total root canal procedure, and should he need it, a surgery like that would take extensive planning. So, the patient was allowed to recover, and for the second time that day, I breathed a deep sigh of relief.

Before we headed for home, the vet took us past the lion enclosure, where up until a year ago – when she moved into a sanctuary – one of their most celebrated animals had resided: a lioness named Emma. Her case came to prominence in 2011. Then thirteen years old and the mother of three cubs, to all intents and purposes, Emma was a normal female lion. Within the space of weeks, however, her keepers noticed she was growing a full and thick mane – typically what a male lion might do at about two years of age. An ultrasound of her abdomen revealed no abnormalities, although a blood test showed that her level of testosterone, which is a predominantly male hormone, was sky high.

A tumour was suspected. Certain types of ovarian tumours can produce testosterone and result in a female 'mascularisation syndrome' – which also occurs in people. It's been known to occur in lions before: much has been written about several wild lionesses with such tumours who've grown manes. Consequently, the decision was made to remove Emma's ovaries. Following the surgery, as expected, her locks fell out and she returned to looking, and likely feeling, like a normal lioness. Where things get complicated, however, is that on pathological examination of her ovaries, no tumour was found, and – in fact – no ovary either. What was supposed to be an ovary had completely turned into a testicle instead – a case that continues to baffle veterinarians today, and remains virtually unheard of in any other animal.

Having experienced far more than we'd bargained for in the space of a single day, around five o'clock we made our weary way back to the farm. It was always a joy to bump along the driveway, now so familiar to me, watching the zebras and giraffes amble through the surrounding scrub as we passed. That evening, like many before, we bush-bashed in the old safari trucks up to the highest point on the property to enjoy the sunset on my final evening in Africa. We toasted it with a beer while watching the colours of the sky change from pink to red, in a show so vibrant that it could only have been the African sky.

In what was a perfect ending to these seemingly endless and life-changing months on a continent that's truly like no other, I received the news that Eric the ostrich had been released into the wild. He'd made a full recovery from his ordeal in the bush – and having had me as a dance partner for the past few weeks. I couldn't have been happier to hear it.

Looking back, my time on the continent shaped me both personally and professionally, far beyond what I could have imagined. While I remained excited for the months ahead, it was bittersweet to know how much was already behind me.

THE AMERICAS

11
Central America

THE FOLLOWING MORNING, as I was frantically repacking my bag, which was almost bursting with all my belongings, I found myself, once more, seriously considering ditching the stones from Zimbabwe. After all, they'd had a nice trip and seen some of Africa, surely they didn't need to come to the Americas as well. Unfortunately, for both my spine and luggage limit, the guilt cropped up again and, for the fifth time in about the same number of months, I reluctantly pushed them back into the bottom of my pack.

My next destination was Costa Rica in Central America, the start of the last leg of my year-long adventure. To get there, I'd made the financially sound yet geographically regrettable decision to fly via Scandinavia and Los

Angeles in what proved to be thirty-eight hours of pure hell. This hell was further compounded on my arrival at Los Angeles International Airport, where I found that the only way to be granted entry *into* Costa Rica was to prove I had a way *out* of it. For a trip that had been meticulously planned up until this point, it seemed I'd dropped the ball spectacularly. The plan for my return journey had been to travel overland from Costa Rica, through Central America and back up to the United States, using local buses, motorbikes and boats. Since none of these required an advance booking, I had no way of proving my onward travel. According to the customs officer, I'd need to find proof – and rather quickly – if I was going to be allowed onto my next flight. Thanks to a mixture of jetlag and the catastrophic level of sleep deprivation I'd accumulated over the past months, I was nursing the mother of all headaches, and found myself poorly equipped to deal with this predicament. Briefly, I strongly considered just giving up and lying face down on the floor but thought better of it and instead retreated to a corner of the airport and attempted to navigate the wi-fi and find a solution to this dilemma. Miraculously, I managed to get online and book a last-minute flight out of the Costa Rican capital of San José, despite having no intention of using it. Almost poetically, the cost of this flight worked out to be close to the exact amount I'd saved by flying through Scandinavia in the first place, although I was in no state to appreciate any irony or humour in this detail at the time.

As I disembarked in Costa Rica, I was knocked sideways by the stifling heat and humidity. It took a number of days to recuperate, which I did at a small, family-owned hostel on the outskirts of San José. From here, my adventure north would take me through the famous cloud forests of the Costa Rican highlands, up the spectacular coastlines of Nicaragua and Honduras, into the mountains of Guatemala, through the tiny Caribbean nation of Belize, and then, finally, to Mexico. From there, I'd be travelling to the United States, where I was due to complete a clinical placement at a large zoo.

I'd arranged my US placement about a year before, with the hope of learning more about the advanced medical treatment of a range of different species, along with the management of their most common ailments. At the time of accepting the position, I was also still entertaining the idea of working as a zoo veterinarian. What better way to contribute to conservation than to use my skills as a veterinarian in this setting? Especially given the extensive work zoos do both within their individual institutions, as well as out in the field.

The time I'd spent in Africa, however, had concentrated my thinking. My eyes had been opened to fresh possibilities available to me as a wildlife vet, or even as a conservationist. I'd been inspired by so many people I'd met on my journey working in a range of capacities – from transporting polar bears in the Arctic Circle, collaborating with governments to combat wildlife trafficking, translocating rhinos and elephants from one part of Africa to the next, working in non-profit organisations to rescue animals from harrowing circumstances, and serving as a wildlife vet in national parks or small, local conservation organisations that operate around the world. I'd also been inspired by the many animals I'd met: Simba and his plight had had a profound effect on me. Although I wasn't yet sure in exactly which field I wished to work, I was strongly drawn to the wilderness – and on my travels I'd been excitedly discovering the details about all kinds of career options I'd never known existed. While I'd never say never, I no longer seriously contemplated working in a zoo. Instead, I now planned to take with me whatever knowledge I'd gained from my experiences back out into the wild as I pursued a path of my own.

The journey north from San José took almost two months to complete, from which a handful of places and encounters left a lasting impact. In saying that, each country had something special or unique to offer. In Costa Rica, I climbed the mountains of Monteverde to reach the awe-inspiring cloud forests that I'd heard so much about. Beneath a shroud of fog, I listened as howler monkeys called out from the treetops, watched anteaters foraging in the low-lying scrub, and marvelled at brightly coloured iguanas basking in the sunlight that filtered through the canopy above. In nearby Guatemala, I scaled a volcano at sunrise and stood on the summit as I watched an adjacent volcano erupt against the backdrop of a vibrant, pink sky; I felt the ground rumbling under my feet and the sand warm from the activity below.

After passing through Nicaragua, I immediately took a twelve-hour overnight bus ride across Honduras, the country's reputation for violent crime and homicide making it an unappealing place to linger.

The island of Utila was the opposite. Located just off the coast, Utila is free from the problems that plague the Honduran mainland. In fact, it's truly a world unto itself. The bus dropped me at the mainland coastal town of La Ceiba, from which I took a short ferry ride over to the island, a paradise of white sandy beaches and clear, turquoise waters. The island is tiny, with one town that you could walk around in the space of half an hour. Were it not jungle, you could probably walk from one side of the island to the other in your lunchtime. It's a place where music rings out, and people warmly greet each other on the street.

This speck in the Caribbean is famed for its diving, natural beauty and, in particular, its resident population of whale sharks. I hoped beyond all else to see these magnificent, ocean-dwelling giants for myself. I'd come at a time of the year when the oceans around Utila are so swamped with them that, during a quick dip in the sea, you could easily find yourself floating among an entire school (or, perhaps, a 'constellation', depending on which collective noun you prefer). With one of them measuring at least 10 metres in length – or about twice that of an elephant, to use an example I was acutely familiar with by this stage – it made for an experience that is impossible to put into words. I remember floating in the clear, warm waters, swimming alongside them and feeling them brush past me with their rough, bumpy skin. Watching them move was like watching a film in slow motion – their huge, spotted forms gracefully glided through the water at a leisurely pace, seemingly without a care in the world.

Beyond the whale sharks, the seas around Utila teemed with life. Dolphins frolicked in the shallows and parrot fish busily chewed on the coral, creating the pristine white sand for which the beaches of the tropics are known. Jellyfish danced on the surface, and turtles lazily drifted by, carried by the current from one spot to the next. As spectacular as each day was, it was the evenings when the real show began. The shorelines and lagoons lit up like a starry sky, illuminated by millions of minute organisms emitting a soft, blue glow in a stunning display of bioluminescence. Triggered by movement, the light display would explode with just a gentle brush of the water with a toe, the throw of a stone, or your body gliding through it in what can only be described as the most extraordinary display of nature I've ever seen.

From its beauty, you could be forgiven for thinking that Utila was a place free from pollution, but as I discovered, this is definitely not so. The surrounding waters, like oceans all over the world, are plagued with what's shaping up to be one of the most urgent issues of our time – microplastics. These are plastic particles measuring less than 5 millimetres in size, either formed by the breakdown of larger plastics or intentionally manufactured for face scrubs, shampoos and toothpastes. At that size, they're often invisible to the naked eye, which enables them to go undetected. Consequently, they're not associated with those all-too-familiar scenes of oceans drowning in Coke bottles and sea life choking on plastic bags. Yet they've been able to permeate almost every corner of the world –

from the top of our highest mountains to the bottom of our deepest oceans. In a recent UK survey, microplastics were detected inside every single marine mammal studied. And, in 2017, another survey found microplastics to be present in tap water around the world.

To say that this matter could be more serious than macroplastic pollution is incredibly difficult to fathom. It's challenging enough to think about the Great Pacific Garbage Patch, a floating conglomeration of plastic waste off the west coast of the United States. At the time of writing, it's three times the size of France, and growing. Even as a vet, having seen and treated turtles with stomachs full of garbage or seabirds strangled by discarded six-pack rings, I find the scale of the macroplastics problem hard to grasp.

But microplastics are becoming one of the gravest threats to our ecosystems and, dare I say it, to us as human beings. While we don't yet know what effects consuming these particles may be having on us, if they're anything like those being seen in marine life around Utila, we should be hugely concerned.

It was issues with filter feeders, like the whale sharks, that first alerted the science community to some of the worrying effects of microplastic ingestion. What researchers found was that microplastics are toxic to the body in large quantities, and they're also capable of wreaking havoc with the hormonal system. Microplastics do this by absorbing organic pollutants from the ocean which, when ingested, can be mistaken by the body as the reproductive hormone oestradiol, due to the pollutants having a similar biological structure. This can cause hormonal disruption in the affected animal and, in extreme cases, lead to the cessation of the reproductive cycle. Should this start to happen in species already on the brink of extinction – for example, in a shrinking population of whale sharks – the effects could be devastating. In fact, marine scientists suspect this process has already begun. Every marine animal tested for the presence of microplastics has returned a positive result, and when you factor in the recent decline in the sharks' reproductive rate, concern is growing about the role these toxic particles are playing.

Although the concept of plastic pollution wasn't new to me, discovering that the damage was far more serious than what we can see was profoundly disturbing. My experiences on Utila have remained at the forefront of my mind over the years since my visit. While I was never an avid consumer of plastics – particularly single-use plastics – it made me re-evaluate some of the choices I make in everyday life. While acknowledging that large-scale and lasting change usually requires action from governing bodies, a lot can be achieved at an individual level with this issue. The choices we make in the supermarket – the brands and products we choose to support – have a direct effect on the environment. Knowing the implications behind those choices has motivated me to change my behaviour.

After two weeks on this small slice of Honduran paradise, and two extensions to my original departure date, I left Utila and its abundance of marine residents to continue my path north. Few things on the journey struck me the way my experiences on the island had, although the ancient Mayan ruins in the jungles of Guatemala were an incredibly humbling sight. From Guatemala, I hopped across to Belize and went up the coast, threading my way between the island 'cayes' – often no more than little uninhabited sandbanks in the middle of the ocean. Once back on the Belize mainland, I made the journey to the Mexican border town of Chetumal.

From the moment I arrived, I found Mexico to be every bit as colourful and welcoming as I'd hoped. Between the ancient ruins, tropical rainforests, beautiful coastlines and rich wildlife, I could have happily stayed there for the rest of the year. I was entranced by the cenotes, which are limestone sinkholes – often found in the middle of the jungle – filled with fresh, piercing blue ground water: a sight that's almost too stunning to believe. Sprawling old tree roots wound their way down the limestone walls, and vines from the branches above dangled into the water, gently rippling the surface and scattering the rays of sunlight in a million different directions. I spent more than one afternoon trekking through the jungle in search of them, before clambering down their steep, treacherous walls, and throwing myself off a rocky ledge into the sparkling water below.

It was easy to think I'd found paradise as I floated on the surface of these cenotes and looked up to the sky above. The breathtaking beauty of the country, in common with many others I'd come across in Africa, was in stark contrast to its dark reputation as a global hotspot of illegal wildlife trafficking. I was all too aware of this reality, especially given its location next to one of the world's largest consumers of illegal wildlife products – the USA. Long known as a country with an insatiable demand for exotic pets and animal products, the States is a key player in the world of wildlife trafficking, with border security apprehending over five *million* individual wildlife parts and products, as well as 660,000 live animals in the past ten years alone. The most in-demand wildlife are exotic birds and fish, pythons and freshwater turtles – making Latin America the perfect supplier, not just due to the convenience of location, but also because of their abundance of wildlife. But that abundance may soon be a thing of the past. In fact, for a region that once had the greatest wildlife diversity on the planet, Latin America has lost an estimated 83 per cent of its animal populations in just the last four decades – largely because of the illegal wildlife trade – which is one of the steepest declines anywhere in the world.

One of the many results of this industry is that veterinarians in Mexico have found themselves on the frontline of a war on wildlife. Traffickers, desperate to get their product into the USA, risk the dangers of swimming across the Rio Grande with boxes full of birds, mammals and reptiles, which are kept afloat by bike tyre inner tubes. Unsurprisingly, many animals die in transit, and others are severely injured. Of the half a million or so animals that were intercepted at the Mexico–US border in the past decade, many ended up in veterinary hospitals, and the vets found themselves tasked with treating all sorts of horrific injuries sustained in the smuggling process. Birds are the most common casualties, often presenting with fractured beaks that, left untreated, render the animal unable to be returned to the wild.

While I'd had little to do with beak injuries myself at the time, it was here in Mexico – my final stop in Latin America – that I connected with some of the vets who had. For an ailment that's often considered almost impossible to treat, particularly when resources are limited, the way these Mexican vets were solving the problem was nothing short of remarkable. Simply put, it was to *print* the patient a new one. To do this, the team from Mexico City – headed by Dr Beremiz Salazar – sought advice from nanotechnology experts and visual artists, and together they came up with a way to use 3D-printing technology to rebuild the lost part of the beak. After some trial and error, several prototypes, and a lot of experimenting with different materials to establish the correct weight and durability, their first patient was a toucan, which was fitted with the prosthesis in 2016. The procedure was done under a general anaesthetic and, within a day, the animal was confidently eating and drinking with his new, bright blue beak in what's since been recognised as a milestone in the treatment of critically injured wildlife.

While this was a unique case at the time, 3D printing has since become widely used in veterinary medicine. Turtles have had new flippers and shells printed after damaging their natural ones in boat strikes, a lizard has received a new foot after losing one to cancer, a new tooth has been printed for a hippopotamus, and there are even teams fighting coral bleaching by creating new, 3D-printed reefs. For me, the toucan remained one of the most remarkable cases I'd heard about, and it inspired me to seek out other vets around the world who are doing pioneering work perfecting treatments that were previously considered impossible. A handful of years later, this took me to a dedicated hospital for elephant amputees in northern Thailand, where they have an entire prosthetics factory on site. Staff there design and build enormous artificial limbs for animals that have lost theirs to landmines, and while these are not 3D-printed, the innovation and sheer magnitude of such an undertaking were truly extraordinary.

12
USA – a far cry from Africa

A COUPLE OF weeks later, my plane was touching down in the USA, the final career-related destination of my journey. It was one of the places I'd been looking forward to most when embarking on this trip close to a year before, thinking that my time in a world-renowned zoo with an equally reputable hospital would be the place I'd learn the most. Within the first few minutes of landing in Africa, however, all those months ago, I had a sneaking suspicion that this assumption had been wildly incorrect.

Around seven the following morning I was standing outside the enormous front gates of the zoo's hospital. It was an entire complex on its own, sitting adjacent to the zoo grounds, and, for a moment, I thought I had the wrong address. By outer appearance, the sprawling, two-storey hospital could have been easily confused for a human one. As I was buzzed through the security gates, the building hummed with activity, even at this early hour. Through the hospital's enormous windows, I could see staff members dressed in scrubs hurrying up and down the hallways, pushing trolleys and drip machines. Outside, an ambulance was being loaded with a selection of medical supplies, and a man walked by with a pager swinging from his belt, a request booming through it for him to make his way to the recovery ward. If I looked carefully, in among the action, there were still a few clues that I'd come to the right place. Off to my left, a young woman was bustling out of the food preparation area, buried in a mountain of leafy branches that were tied together with a label that read 'Koalas'. Inside a small room off to the side, another woman was tending to what appeared to be a lemur, and in front of me a man was tearing off in a golf buggy with a dart gun flung over his shoulder.

The parking area was filled with designated spots for the veterinarians and specialists who worked inside – their titles made for an impressive but intimidating sight. I waited out the front of the building for the director of the hospital to arrive, feeling out of place as I did. If one thing was certain, it was that I definitely wasn't in

Africa anymore. Suddenly, I felt very self-conscious about the ill-fitting pants I'd picked up from Target on my way from the airport, and the cheap shirt that squeaked every time I moved my arms. I felt like a fish out of water – a bumbling new graduate standing in the carpark of a first-class institution full of esteemed and highly qualified experts. Just as I began to entertain the idea of allowing full-blown panic to set in, the director popped his head out of the door beside me and gestured me inside.

The first thing I noticed, as I stood in the well-lit but somewhat cold and sterile room, was the speed at which things operated. There were people everywhere I turned, and running seemed to be the new walking. Maybe I'd been in Africa too long, where anything more than a stroll was considered a frantic pace at which to work. In saying that, there were, of course, a few notable exceptions to this, the rhino incident being one of them.

The director introduced himself, along with a few of the other members of staff as they flew by, and we began my orientation in the largest room of the hospital – the one in which we were standing – the preparation area. It was a vast open space with an extensive pharmacy to one side, a small operating table in the middle, an anaesthetic machine behind it, a row of surgical sinks along the back wall, and two sliding glass doors that opened to individual, fully equipped surgical suites. These suites had enormous padded operating tables, the size of the ones in the equine hospital back at university, and were clearly built to accommodate some of the zoo's larger patients. On the walls, a series of photo boards displayed some of the more memorable procedures that had been performed here, a few of which caught my eye as we continued the tour at what I'd call a slow jog. From what I could see, there appeared to be an orangutan undergoing cataract surgery; a young giraffe, seemingly born with a limb deformity, having corrective splints placed; a gorilla undergoing a caesarian; and a huge saltwater crocodile lying on the operating table – mouth propped wide open – as a vet removed one of its teeth.

A bit further along from the preparation room, down a small hallway, was the intensive care unit. It was filled with a series of humidicribs and oxygen machines, typically used in the care of neonates and critical patients. Adjacent to this was a recovery ward, designed to accommodate the animals waking up from surgery, and sure enough, the man with the pager I'd seen outside was in here tending to a penguin. As we continued down the hallway, we came to the imaging room, which was fitted with an X-ray machine and ultrasound scanner. The zoo, like many others, also had access to an MRI machine, although given it was housed in the local human medical clinic, the zoo's use was strictly limited to evenings. After all, it was unlikely to be received well if a member of the public found themselves second in line to an orangutan. Finally, at the end of the hallway was a firearms room, equipped with more dart guns that I'd come across during my entire time in Africa, and a large laboratory that was packed with sophisticated equipment that beeped, clanked and hummed as we passed.

At the end of the tour, I was taken upstairs to meet the veterinary team that I'd be shadowing for the next two months. I found myself in a sizeable area with several offices clustered at one end, a library at the other and a large meeting room in the middle, where morning rounds were held each day at 7.30 am. I was introduced to the two veterinarians I'd be working alongside – an older one, who'd served as the zoo's head vet for the past thirty years, and another who wasn't much older than me, just starting out himself. While jobs in the zoo are usually hard to come by, and commonly require the applicant to have completed a gruelling three-year residency training program, not every zoo vet goes down this path. The younger vet had been hired after spending a few years as a general practitioner in the area, while also spending his weekends volunteering at the zoo. While he didn't have the board certification that a residency provides, he'd become eligible to sit the specialist exams after six years of working within the zoo itself.

After meeting the team, I was handed a uniform – a scrub top and cargo pants, a vast improvement on my failed attempt at professional attire à la Target. It was nearing the time for morning rounds, so we all gathered in the meeting room to discuss the patients of the day, along with some of the procedures that had been scheduled for the week. I was handed a large print-out containing the medical records of each patient that was due to be seen by the veterinary team. It was a frighteningly comprehensive document, and I was duly impressed by the daily case-load. They seemed to have one of everything – from a sick baby stingray (rather charmingly known as a pup) in the ICU that needed to be syringe-fed every day, to a rhino that was receiving laser therapy following surgery to remove a cancer in its horn. The latter certainly piqued my interest, as I couldn't say that I'd ever seen something like that before. Further down the list, a flock of recently hatched flamingos were due for their first vaccinations, and a tapir was undergoing a modified form of dialysis to correct a disorder of its blood. If you've never seen one before, a tapir can best be described as a giant, black-and-white pig, mixed with a touch of elephant, given the fact that it has a small trunk.

The meeting concluded with the senior vet giving a summary of recent cases that had been resolved, including – although I thought I'd misheard for a moment – a polar bear that had turned electric *green*. I nearly laughed, thinking he was trying to break up the seriousness of the room with some light-hearted veterinary humour, only to be deeply thankful a moment later that I hadn't. Polar bears changing colour is a common occurrence, from white and grey to green, orange, yellow, or even purple. In fact, in a detail that had escaped me up until that moment, the famously white Arctic bears are actually black. Well, their skin is, at least, in a nifty trick to absorb the sunlight and keep them warm. The hairs on top, however, are transparent hollow tubes, reflecting the light to make them, normally, appear white. In different lights, say at sunset, they can reflect the glow of the sun to appear orange, or, in the case of many polar bears living in warmer climates, algae can take up residence inside the hollow hairs to make them look green. The treatment for this is a bath in salt water or peroxide, and the condition resolves itself in a matter of days – just as it had done in the case they'd discussed here.

By the time we left the meeting, I'd gathered that the tone of the place was one of polite formality. For me, this required an adjustment after my experiences in Africa, and I got the feeling that several of my escapades during that time wouldn't be considered appropriate conduct here. Firstly, I was doubtful that the funny side would be seen if I turned up to work one day accidentally dressed as a zebra – not that I'd seen the funny side of it myself at the time. It was also extremely unlikely that I'd be left to my own devices with an ostrich. Mind you, after reflecting on my experiences with Eric (as well as viewing a few YouTube videos of ostriches gone bad), I'd become more forgiving of myself: that had been a disaster waiting to happen. Then again, there's usually an upside to most situations. The main one I could see here was that, given the extensive pharmacy on the floor below, it was extremely unlikely that an animal's access to medication would hinge on my ability to convince a human pharmacist to dispense it, a great improvement on my time in Malawi.

Most days, the morning rounds were followed by a visit to the zoo to check in with the keepers about any sick or recovering animals. During this time, we were also able to perform any treatments done outside of the hospital, such as the laser therapy on the rhino or the dialysis on the tapir. On this first day, however, for a reason I can't remember, the vets were occupied in the office for the first few hours of the morning and, instead, I was given my first solo assignment out in the zoo.

To call it a solo assignment gives an air of importance to the task that is, in fact, a touch misleading. I'll rephrase. What I'd actually been tasked with was something that I'd incorrectly interpreted as a joke for the second time in about twenty minutes. I was initially excited about the prospect of having a job to do, and had been summoned into the senior vet's office to collect a parcel that I'd be needing for it. When I got there, I was greeted with the sight of a giant, cylindrical container sitting on his desk, which he quickly bundled up and handed to me. He then asked if I could deliver it to the giraffe-keepers, and while there, if I could collect the stool sample with glitter in it. In that moment, I'd thought that I'd either seriously misheard him, was starting to hallucinate from sleep deprivation, or that he was pulling my leg. I searched his expression for a hint of cheek, waiting for the corners of his mouth to turn up and burst into a laugh – a real 'gotcha' moment – but it never came. Considering it was my first day, I decided not to push my luck and instead accepted the container without further question.

As I left his office, still unsure about what had just happened, curiosity got the better of me and I unscrewed the lid. Sure enough, it was filled with glitter. Silver glitter, to be exact, and about 3 kilograms of it. I hauled the container downstairs with me, threw it onto the back of the golf cart and took off into the zoo, mentally calculating where on the list of strangest things of the year this would sit. I was also trying to contemplate what on earth a giraffe-keeper would need with 3 kilograms of glitter, or any glitter at all for that matter, and what it would be doing in an animal's stools.

The giraffe-keepers seemed to have been expecting me, or, more accurately, their box of glitter. One of the keepers launched into an explanation. I followed him over to the feeding station, where each giraffe had their own food bowl, and watched as he poured the glitter all over one labelled 'Emily'. As it turned out, Emily was part of their breeding herd of giraffes, and to establish when she was most likely to fall pregnant, her stools were being analysed for hormone levels. To know which ones were hers in a group of seven, she was being fed hay smothered in glitter, creating an extremely unusual treasure hunt for the keepers each morning as they scoured the enclosure for her samples. Suddenly, it all made sense and, once again I thanked my lucky stars that I hadn't laughed in response to a serious comment. In fact, it was around this point I made a silent pact with myself to think long and hard before laughing about anything ever again, no matter how inviting the scenario. At least while I was here.

That day, and most of those that followed, I arrived back from the zoo grounds (glittery sample in tow) to find that multiple calls had come through from keepers, each with a different concern or query about one of their animals. A diabetic gorilla hadn't eaten his breakfast, so the keepers had been unable to deliver his insulin, a lemur had landed awkwardly from a jump and now wasn't bearing weight on its left leg, a seal with a history of heart disease was looking unwell, and a pregnant François' langur – a species of monkey – had just given birth two weeks early. These calls would be fielded between tending to the patients who were already on the list of cases for the day – a hungry baby stingray and a flock of young flamingos – and prioritised in order of urgency. For greater efficiency, the two vets divided the cases between them and, having had enough surprises from the older one that day, I decided to join the younger one on the call-out to the seal, the lemur and the langur monkey.

We prioritised the langur, not only because she'd given birth prematurely, but also because it was her first time at parenthood. This increased the chances of her rejecting her newborn, meaning that a swift intervention would be necessary to support the baby through the first few weeks of life. As with most newborns – whether they depend on their parents in their first weeks, months or even years of life – the first two days of this period are some of the most critical. It's during this time that, just like human babies, animals receive a vital nutrient from their mother's milk, known as colostrum. It contains proteins from their mother's immune system that will protect them until they're old enough to develop one of their own. Given our concerns about abandonment, and what it could mean for the infant, we loaded one of the humidicribs into the ambulance and set off for their enclosure.

As we approached, I could see the newborn from a mile away. After all, that's how François' langur babies were designed. Unlike their parents, which have unique characteristics of their own, langur offspring are bright orange balls of fluff – a trait that helps their mothers find them in the thick, dark forests of their native countries, China and Vietnam. As they grow older, the orange hair falls out, and they transform into long and slender, black-haired adults, with some distinctive – and impressive – white sideburns that run along their cheekbones. The unique appearance of both adults and young has made them a target for poachers and traffickers, who are able to sell them to the exotic pet industry for a considerable price. Along with a significant amount of habitat loss in recent years, this practice has sadly seen their numbers in the wild fall to a meagre one thousand individuals – making the animal before me a critically endangered being.

It was plain to see that the mother had no interest in her young. And, while this was neither uncommon nor unexpected from a first-time mother, it was disappointing news. Hand-rearing an animal is fraught with complications and is never the outcome that's hoped for among keepers and veterinarians. It is, however, necessary in these cases of abandonment, the importance of which is heightened even further for a species whose survival in the wild is far from guaranteed. We wasted no time in bundling up the young langur and performing a quick clinical exam to ascertain her health status, as well as to check if she'd sustained any injuries during birth. Luckily, she hadn't, although she was becoming hypothermic from her time on the ground. An on-the-spot blood test to measure her glucose levels also revealed that she was low in energy, so sugar was applied to her gums and she was placed in the humidicrib for warming and oxygen support. Because these young animals are primed to cling to their mothers at this early stage of life, we'd also come prepared with a black-and-white teddy. As soon as this was handed to her, she latched onto it – the start of a friendship that would continue for weeks to come. With the utmost care, we carried back the humidicrib and its special cargo to the ambulance for the trip to the hospital, where the newborn would receive ongoing, around-the-clock care in the neonatal ward until she was fit enough to be returned to her group.

After this, the rest of the day was remarkably easier than how it had started. The giraffe had its glitter, I'd been educated on the fact the polar bears can turn whatever colour they like, the young François' langur was safe in the hospital, the stingray was fed, the flamingos were vaccinated, and we only had two patients left on our list – the seal and the lemur. In fact, that afternoon was smooth sailing, although I'm sure the lemur would have disagreed. A quick X-ray of his leg revealed that the bone was, indeed, broken, so a splinted bandage was put in place, and he was scheduled to have it repaired in surgery the following morning. As for the seal, she was a dream to work with. Given her history of heart disease – something for which these animals are predisposed – we'd taken the ultrasound machine to her pool to assess her heart function, and found her waiting by the gate for us when we arrived.

As I soon discovered, the zoo had done a lot of work in conditioning some of the more intelligent species to participate in medical examinations without the need for sedation, and the seals were one of them. The gorillas were another. They'd learned to sit still while their blood pressure was measured, and even to hold out their arm for blood sampling. Not only does this practice benefit the patient by removing the stress of darting, in many instances – such as that of measuring blood pressure – it facilitates a more accurate reading. Most importantly, it's also much safer. It eliminates the risks associated with sedating or anaesthetising an animal. The harder it is to do – and some species are notoriously difficult to sedate – the greater those risks. Seals are some of the most challenging species to work with – their ability to hold their breath for extended periods under water makes their anaesthesia uniquely complex, particularly with drugs that have to be inhaled to be effective. Then there's their extremely confronting odour, although admittedly, this is slightly beside the point being made here. Coming back to the anaesthesia, there are, of course, ways to navigate the difficulties associated with it; however, having a patient that's able to float on their back while we examine them, as we had now, made all the difference. In fact, she may have just been one of the most relaxed animals I'd ever seen. To our relief, we found no evidence of worsening heart disease on the scan, and she was able to return to her pool with an all-clear from us.

Most days at the zoo continued along this trajectory. A flurry of patients and surprises, a blur of activity and a lot of running. But one day, things took a distinctly different path. It was about halfway through my time at the zoo, and I arrived bright and early to find two people lingering around the hospital, dressed head-to-toe as tigers. Tired from a lack of sleep – thanks in part to my landlord, Barbara, watching 1970s sitcoms on her television into the early hours of the morning with the volume turned up high – I didn't think much of this strange sight. By the time lunch rolled around, it had left my mind altogether. Then, somewhere around one o'clock, as I was checking in with the young langur, an alarm sounded in the hospital. The words 'code red' started booming loudly over the speakers, a message that echoed through the radios and pagers. If I thought people had been running beforehand, I was sorely mistaken. The hospital exploded with activity and, in the blink of an eye, about twenty people were gathered in the hallway outside the room where I was tending to the langur. With a distinct look of alarm on their faces, they hurriedly started gathering supplies and, from what I saw being collected – nets, dart guns, drugs, ropes, stretchers – I began to suspect that there'd been an escape.

Swept up in the action, I soon found myself clinging to the back of a golf cart as we tore off into the zoo. The scene vividly reminded of my time in Zimbabwe and was a bizarre parallel to many of my experiences there. As we rocketed over the speed bumps, I could hear nearby police sirens, which were getting louder by the second. Red – as it turned out – was the code for a dangerous animal escape, reserved for the most threatening of species. As we raced up the main strip of the zoo, visitors were being rushed to the exits, and keepers were blocking off all exit and entry points to the area of interest. We sped through the barricades, my heart thumping heavily in my chest with anticipation of what lay ahead. I couldn't help but notice how horrifically – almost to the point of laughably, had it not been so serious – unprepared I was for such a thing and started to wonder why I'd jumped on the golf cart in the first place. It was only once we rounded the corner, heading towards the elephant houses, that I caught sight of the two culprits and remembered my morning encounter. Suddenly, it dawned on me. It was a drill. The cart came to a screeching halt, the vet clambered onto the roof, dart gun in hand, and five keepers charged the pair of 'tigers' with a net, entangling them on the ground. A cheer erupted among the group as everyone celebrated their success; even the pair under the netting managed to find a way to high-five each other in congratulations of a job well done.

It turns out that most major zoos worldwide are required to perform several of these drills each year, to ensure they are adequately prepared in the event of a real escape. Although most zoos participate in these drills, the level of commitment to them seems to differ from region to region. In fact, if I thought ours had been extreme, it only took a quick Google search to learn that, in Japan, they take things to a whole other level. It's there that they have a giant, to-scale, papier mâché rhinoceros charge at groups of bewildered and, I imagine, terrified schoolchildren while the army, police and fire departments are called in to intervene. This contrasts with some other parts of the world, where an escape drill is more along the lines of someone walking around with the word 'elephant' on their T-shirt. Then again, the level of danger does vary according to where you are on the globe. In Japan, a country fraught with frequent and devastating earthquakes, the risk of damage to facilities and the subsequent escape of animals is a very real possibility. Other places, such as the zoo in China that, in 2013, got sprung passing off a group of large, hairy dogs as lions in their lion exhibit, perhaps have less to worry about – at least when it comes to a lion escape.

There was no doubt I saw a range of weird and wonderful things during my time at the zoo, reaffirming my first impressions that this experience would be a formative one in my career, albeit with a steep learning curve. Between learning that glitter could be used as a medical aid, discovering that polar bears are essentially transparent, and experiencing exactly what an escape drill entails, it was quickly becoming two months to remember. Looking back at this time, despite the blur of animals that it had become, there is one that remains at the forefront of my mind: a tapir named Benjamin.

I met Benjamin on my second day in the zoo and spent many afternoons with him over the course of my stay. He was the tapir I'd learned about on my first day in rounds who was having regular dialysis treatment for his iron disorder. While I knew little to nothing about tapirs before meeting him, I came away with a newfound appreciation for this species, but above all for Benjamin. I don't know what it was about him, perhaps that we were similar in age – he was twenty-five and I was twenty-six – or that we both enjoyed having a good relax in the sun, but we really hit it off and developed an instant rapport.

On the day we met, I'd entered his enclosure at around two in the afternoon, armed with a bag full of blood-sampling equipment and a garden rake. If Benjamin was surprised to see the rake, it was nothing on what I was feeling, especially when I'd been told it was all I'd be needing to 'sedate' him. While I was aware that the vet who'd briefed me hadn't been referring to a *medical* sedation with drugs – the kind I'd become all too familiar with in Africa – I wasn't sure exactly *what* he was referring to. From what I could tell from looking at him, Benjamin had some frighteningly large canine teeth and I couldn't quite see how the rake was going to help me should he decide to sink one of them into my thigh.

A rake really was all I'd be needing to keep him still for the procedure. It was a pseudo-sedation of sorts, which all came down to something known as the vagal response. This response depends on a nerve in the body responsible for relaxation, the vagus nerve. All vertebrates, including humans, have this nerve, and if you know how to stimulate it, you can trigger a profound relaxation, which, in some species, can be so extreme that it almost appears as if the animal is sedated. I was already aware of this phenomenon in reptiles, which is achieved with some light pressure on the eyelids, although some astute people will point out that this still doesn't solve the issue of *getting* to the eyelids – especially if the reptile in question happens to be a 4-metre-long saltwater crocodile. In humans, the vagus nerve is stimulated by taking long, deep breaths, which also happens to be one of the reasons this is the first advice given to someone who is stressed or anxious.

In tapirs, as I learned with Benjamin, their sweet spot is the sides – hence the rake. Before going into their enclosure, a quick scratch along their body with the rake will often be enough to induce a relaxation response so deep they'll collapse onto the ground and stay there, so long as you continue to scratch. In fact, with just two people – one of them being a full-time scratcher – it's possible to do almost anything you'd like with them in this state. This trick was incredibly useful when treating Benjamin's condition, which required us to spend up to an hour at a time with him. His disorder was known as iron storage disease, a genetic condition reported most commonly in humans, tapirs, black rhinos and lemurs – a rather unusual bunch. It often arises when the cells of the body are unable to metabolise excess iron, resulting in it accumulating in the bloodstream and tissues, leading to a dangerous condition known as haemochromatosis. Should this be left untreated, there are several possible outcomes, of which none are remotely appealing. The worst of them is organ failure, caused by the build-up of iron in the tissues. Another is diabetes, following injury to the pancreas, along with an increased risk of cancer, given that iron is a known promoter of cancerous cells. Because of this, the treatment of choice is repeated bleedings, known as serial phlebotomies, carried out so as to remove as much excess iron from the body as possible.

While this wasn't great news for Benjamin, it was encouraging to watch how well he tolerated these treatments. Spending these extended periods of time with him was also a joy for me. As a vet in a zoo, it's not often that you're able to spend long stretches with your patients, and certainly not while they're awake. Benjamin was an exception to this, and my experiences with him were every bit as special as those with Eric in South Africa, and with Simba and Bella in Malawi. I have particularly fond memories of these animals, no doubt as a result of having the privilege of getting to know their individual personalities and quirks. From two lions that were very relaxed and placid, one ostrich that was much less so, and a tapir who was somewhere in between, they'd all left their mark on me in different ways – and the same can be said of my time in the zoo.

Despite having suspected at the outset of this experience that a career in a zoo was probably not for me, I came away with an overwhelming respect for everything zoos do, the collective knowledge of their team and their passion for conservation. And, last but not least, a newfound love of tapirs.

AND NOW?

13
The good news stories

As I write this, it has been five years since my graduation as a veterinarian. In that time, I've witnessed the career progression of many friends and colleagues, most of whom are working as general practitioners in local veterinary clinics. For a couple of years, I did some of those things, too. After returning from America via the Galapagos Islands – where I saw the giant tortoises, some of the oldest animals on the planet – I went on to complete a year-long internship. That was pretty gruelling. Following this, I spent a bit of time in general practice, developing my skills as a vet by treating a range of household pets, including in Scotland. That's where I tried my hand at emergency work, and it proved to be every bit as stressful as the name suggests. As fate would have it, I met another vet, and in 2018 we married. Throughout all these adventures, my love of life in the wild – and desire to do more of that work – has remained undimmed. But I certainly don't look at life as a 'jungle doctor' through rose-coloured glasses.

Optimism can, at times, be in short supply when it comes to the natural world. For this reason alone, being a wildlife vet can be emotionally taxing. Seeing rhinos that have had their horns and faces unceremoniously hacked off with chainsaws before being left for dead by the side of the road – for nothing but a glorified fingernail – can be tough. I've met lions plucked from the most horrific of circumstances, after suffering years of abuse at the hands of humans. I think of the monkeys that had been kept chained to poles and hit with sticks for fun, giraffes that had been trapped in snares and burned alive for bush meat, and elephants that had been shot so that their tusks could be harvested while they were left to die a slow and painful death. Meanwhile, I've learned that our sea life is not only drowning in plastic, it's being poisoned by it too.

The bad news continues. In the past few years, Maasai giraffes have been declared endangered in what's being referred to as a silent extinction of the species. Demand for wildlife and wildlife products – such as pet macaws, pangolin scales, and bile harvested from the gall bladders of Asiatic black bears – is thought to be on the rise. In 2018, the USA lifted a longstanding ban on the importation of African elephant trophies, fuelling a resurgence in both the legal and illegal hunting of these magnificent creatures, and their *Endangered Species Act* has been drastically weakened. For the first time, the Act has allowed economic factors to be taken into consideration – for instance, estimating lost revenue from a ban on mining in a critical habitat – when deciding whether a species warrants protection or not. Elsewhere in the world, Iran's radical regime continues to suppress environmental groups and imprison conservationists – accusing them of spying and 'corruption on the earth', both crimes that carry the death penalty. Many Asian countries continue to allow the sale of critically endangered animals through their notorious wet markets, and in China the use of rhino horn and tiger bones in traditional medicines is still being promoted.

Aside from the human factor – that is, our unique ability to decimate the natural world and the species that inhabit it – our climate is changing too. With this comes a range of implications. In 2019, we watched in horror as the Amazon rainforest, the unofficial home of our planet's wildlife and biodiversity, was ravaged by fire – devastating already fragile populations of South American wildlife.

Then, in early 2020, the same thing happened in Australia and I found myself on the frontline of the recovery efforts, treating badly burned native animals in some of the most confronting scenes I've witnessed.

Despite these catastrophic events – ones that have far-reaching consequences for us all – our priorities as a society don't seem to reflect the urgent response required. Three months after the catastrophe in the Amazon, the Notre-Dame cathedral in Paris caught alight. Before the blaze had even been extinguished, hundreds of millions of dollars had been pledged for its restoration, a figure that grew, within a week, to more than a billion dollars. Overnight, media coverage across the world exploded with the news, and the financial contributions dwarfed those received for the Amazon and Australia combined.

While Notre-Dame was a tragic loss, I couldn't help but think about the loss of our other treasures – ones that can never be rebuilt. The forests, the coral reefs, the rich biodiversity of our planet. Just two days before the Notre-Dame fire, the last female Yangtze River turtle died, and with it, her species. This turtle had roamed the Earth for millions of years, and unlike Notre-Dame, there was no hope for its return. Meanwhile, the forests in Borneo continued to be cleared at the rate of eight football fields a minute, taking with them the orangutans – one of our closest relatives. These forests, which have been standing for 140 million years, have been replaced with palm oil plantations – vast monocultures that, among other things, have been found to absorb almost no carbon dioxide from the atmosphere, permanently altering the air we breathe. The sixth mass extinction of our planet – the one in which we currently live – rages on as we continue to lose biodiversity at an unprecedented rate. To me, however, the world doesn't seem too concerned about these natural treasures, the ones on which we depend for our very survival. The amount of media coverage and funding pale in relation to the significance of these losses, and globally, governments have repeatedly failed to make a meaningful commitment to addressing them. Worst of all, Australia is leading the charge. Here, a combination of inaction, ambivalence and a seeming inability to implement an effective species recovery plan has seen us become the country with the highest rate of mammal extinction in the world.

But there are good news stories too. It's these that I choose to focus on, and they are the ones that inspire me – along with the people behind them. For example, largely thanks to scientists, researchers and conservationists, tiger numbers are on the rise in India for the first time since the 1980s. The same can be said of the South Atlantic humpback whale – a species that was decimated by commercial whaling in the twentieth century. Since the ban on whaling, their population has bounced back from just 440 individuals in the 1950s to over 20,000 today. It's hoped that vaquitas – the smallest porpoises in the world – will share a similar trajectory. Just a metre in length, these marine mammals are not only the smallest of their kind but also the rarest, with only roughly ten individuals remaining in the wild. They're collateral damage from the lucrative market for traditional medicines, as fishermen anchor nets to the ocean floor to catch another endangered species – the totoaba, whose valuable swim bladders are illegally traded to China, where they are used in treating various ailments. As the vaquitas become trapped in these nets, they suffocate and drown. It's a practice that has destroyed the species, but in late 2019, a mother with calves was sighted off the coast of Mexico – renewing hope for their survival. And, of course, it would be remiss of me not to mention the mountain gorillas. At the time of my visit, they'd become the only great ape species in the world whose numbers were rising – a true testament to the tireless efforts of the rangers and conservationists who risk their lives daily to protect them.

Perhaps one of the most uplifting stories of all is of a Bolivian frog called Romeo. A Sehuencas water frog,

Romeo was feared to be the last of his kind. He'd been collected from the wild in 2009, in the hope of then finding a mate and establishing a captive breeding population – in case his species became extinct. Despite the team's best efforts, however, subsequent searches for more Sehuencas water frogs came up empty-handed, and Romeo spent many long years in solitude, croaking for a mate.

Eventually, he fell silent. With limited funding for the search to continue, Romeo's team prepared themselves for the seeming inevitability that he would die alone, which would signal the end of his species. In a last-ditch effort, on Valentine's Day 2018, they set up a Match.com profile for Romeo, and suddenly his luck changed. The public, eager to see Romeo find a partner, donated $25,000 for the search to continue, and after weeks scouring every nook and cranny of the Bolivian cloud forests for his Juliet, they found her. A few weeks later, Juliet moved in to Romeo's aquarium and, not long after that, Romeo croaked for the first time since 2017 – a sign he was ready to mate. The pair remain the last chance for their species, and if this sign is anything to go by, there's still hope yet.

Good stories like these are the ones I want to be a part of. During my year abroad, I'd already come across a few of my own: the mountain gorillas in Uganda and Simba in Malawi are two of the more notable cases. In the years since, I've continued to seek out veterinarians and conservationists doing exceptional pioneering work. Through this, I've met people working tirelessly to make a difference, not just for entire species, but in the lives of individual animals. The team building prosthetic limbs for elephants injured by landmines is one of these examples.

Another came a few years later when I learned about the people revolutionising the way we treat animals that have been badly burned in bushfires.

This team was the first to use a novel biological bandage that's been found to speed the healing process and provide excellent pain relief at the same time – it's made from the skin of a fish. Specifically, this is the tilapia fish, which is abundant in Brazil. This unique and effective way to treat burns patients has since been used in both human and veterinary medicine, including in Australia. It's these people, and developments like this, that inspire me to this day.

My own return to the wild happened sooner than expected. Alongside building up my experiences in practice, both at home and abroad, I've continued to contribute my time to different wildlife organisations wherever possible. This is how I found myself working alongside a small Tanzanian organisation dedicated to teaching school students about conservation matters in their country. Drawing on the work I'd done in East Africa, I helped to design programs to take students from rural Maasai villages on safaris to see their country's wildlife for the first time. It was my hope that these experiences would provide an opportunity for them to engage and connect with 'their' animals, and perhaps even inspire some to champion wildlife protection one day.

This theme runs through my ongoing work on the frontline of wildlife conservation, as a veterinarian, and indeed my current role, which is one I feel lucky to have. This involves taking high school and university students from around the world along with me as I collaborate with remarkable people from all walks of life who share my passions. I hope to showcase the range of extraordinary work being done in the field of conservation, and impart to these students something that was instilled in me from a young age – that a career can be anything you wish to make it, however unconventional the path. And, as I reflect on how this role evolved for me, there's no doubt that much stemmed from my year in Africa and the Americas.

As with most things in life, that time hadn't been without its frustrations. After all, I had lugged about three kilograms of stones around with me for the better part of a year! That wasn't something I'd forget in a hurry. There were many moments when I'd considered getting rid of them, yet I brought them back to Australia and felt a sense of accomplishment that I hadn't succumbed to that, at times, overwhelming temptation.

On the day of my arrival, I wearily lowered myself to the ground, shrugged off my pack and gratefully pulled the damn things out for the final time. Triumphantly, I presented them to the geologist in question – my dad – and sat waiting, with bated breath, for him to tell me what they were. His response was going to make up for all the months those eighteen stones had weighed me down on my travels. My father took one look at the stones, one look at me, and paused before summing up his thoughts succinctly: 'Wouldn't have a clue.'

Epilogue

When sitting down to write this book, it was my intention to highlight – in equal parts – my concern for the natural world, as well as my awe and wonder for it. Sometime during the process, I came across a poem that resonated with me. It beautifully articulates the message I hope my readers will take away.

Do not be dismayed by the brokenness of the world.
All things break. And all things can be mended.
Not with time, as they say, but with intention.
So go. Love intentionally, extravagantly, unconditionally.
The broken world waits in darkness for the light
that is you.
– L.R. Knost

I want *The Jungle Doctor* to be a book of optimism and hope. A reminder that, despite the brokenness we see in so many parts of the environment, not all is lost.

Undoubtedly, the time for action is now. Be assured that there is a role for everyone in conservation – scientists, yes, but also artists, lawmakers, teachers, strategists, tech gurus, gig workers, CEOs, entrepreneurs, homemakers, writers, agriculturalists, students, explorers, aunts and uncles ... People who care enough to recognise that we cannot continue to neglect and exploit the very thing that sustains us. People who are crazy enough to think they can change the world for the better – in my limited experience, they are usually the ones who do just that.

Through the culmination of many small steps and conscious actions, I believe a brighter future can be had for the natural world, and by extension, for us all.

I would like to express my sincere gratitude for your purchase of this book. I will be donating 100 per cent of my author royalties to a selection of wildlife conservation organisations around the world. Thank you for your support.

Acknowledgements

WHILE I HAVE MANY people to thank for making this book a reality, I'd like to start with my mum, Wendy, who gave me a unique, exciting and happy childhood filled with awe and wonder. Thank you for instilling in me the confidence to believe I was capable of achieving my dreams and aspirations in life, and for hammering into me the importance of doing 'good', as well as 'well'. It would be remiss of me not to also thank you for being my unofficial editor-in-chief, waging your war on commas, hyphens and 'Gen-Y' spelling. This book is because of you, in more ways than one. I love you with all my heart.

To my husband, Jan, the most patient and supportive man in the world, who salvaged this book from a late-night meltdown on more than one occasion and who has now read every chapter so many times that I'm sure they must haunt him in his sleep. When you came into my life, it was the best thing that ever happened to me, and I still pinch myself every day.

My grandmother, Mary, or to me simply 'Dar', who, at 96 years of age, passed away just as this was going to print. We shared a very special bond, and I will take you with me in my heart wherever I go. How can two people be so much alike? Much to Mum's dismay, I'm sure. I have so much to thank you for, Dar, and I love you more than I can say.

To Rob – a loving, reassuring and unwavering presence in my life since day one.

To my dad, Robert, sisters Abby and Jess, and to my friends who may as well be sisters, too. As clichéd as it sounds, friends are the family you make for yourself, and this is certainly true of mine. To Nikki, Kate and Loren – the ridiculousness of vet school ensured we developed an unbreakable bond. Even if I'd never gone on to become a vet at the end of it all, it still would have been worth it for meeting you. And to my dearest friends Caitlin and Rachel – you know far too much about me; rest assured I'll always keep you close.

To the entire team at Pantera Press. Thank you for believing in this book and working tirelessly to turn what felt like a far-fetched dream into a reality. An extra special mention to Marty, who has become a good friend since our unconventional first meeting in Scotland all those years ago, and Anne, who supported me throughout the entire process.

And finally, to the nature lovers I dedicated this book to … This includes all conservationists – past, present and future – and my colleagues in the veterinary profession: there are far too many to name individually. I am inspired by your dedication, passion and commitment to this field, and am proud to share this profession with you. Thank you for welcoming me into it and for sharing your knowledge with me.

Chloe Buiting is an Australian veterinarian and wildlife conservationist. Her experience growing up on Australia's beautiful Lord Howe Island inspired her to pursue a career in the field of wildlife conservation.

Chloe completed a Bachelor of Science and Doctor of Veterinary Medicine, both at the University of Melbourne. Following this, she undertook additional training in large-animal anaesthesia in Africa. Chloe has since spent time working and volunteering with a range of wildlife organisations around the world.

Chloe shares her adventures on Instagram as @jungle_doctor, and through her website jungledoctor.org. When she isn't working abroad, she lives with her husband Jan (who is also a wildlife vet!) on Kangaroo Island in South Australia. They enjoy surfing, snorkelling, hanging out with friends and, of course, looking after the orphaned kangaroo joeys that come into their care!